The Sports Connection

MW01236127

Integrated Simulation

Microsoft® Office 2003

Susie H. VanHuss, Ph.D.

Executive Director of University Foundations
Distinguished Professor Emeritus
University of South Carolina

•

Connie M. Forde, Ph.D.

Professor, Department of Instructional Systems,
Leadership, and Workforce Development
Mississippi State University

THOMSON
SOUTH-WESTERN

Australia · Brazil · Canada · Mexico · Singapore · Spain · United Kingdom · United States

THOMSON

SOUTH-WESTERN

The Sports Connections, Integrated Simulation: Microsoft® Office 2003, 3E

Susie H. VanHuss and Connie M. Forde

VP/Editorial Director
Jack W. Calhoun

VP/Editor-in-Chief
Karen Schmohe

VP, Director of Marketing
Carol Volz

Acquisitions Editor
Jane Phelan

Project Manager
Karen Hein

Consulting Editor
Dianne Rankin

Marketing Manager
Valerie A. Lauer

Production Project Manager
Colleen A. Farmer

Manufacturing Coordinator
Charlene Taylor

Production House
GGS Book Services

Printer
Banta Company, Harrisonburg

Art Director
Stacy Shirley

Internal Designer
Kathy Heming

Cover Designer
Kathy Heming

Front Cover Photo Credit
© Getty Images

For more information about our products, contact us at:

Thomson Higher Education
5191 Natorp Boulevard
Mason, Ohio 45040
USA

Go Beyond the Basics

Explore these other opportunities to integrate the latest technology! Whether you are looking for comprehensive texts, brief units of instruction, or technology-based applications, South-Western has the material to fill all of your needs.

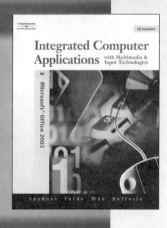

Integrated Computer Applications 4E

Build on essential word-processing skills and reinforce communication, keyboarding, and Internet skills while learning all the tools of Microsoft® Office. Coverage includes the basics of Excel, Access, Outlook, and PowerPoint® and the integration of these applications with Word documents. Organized into distinct modules for custom learning needs.

Module 1	Business Documents with Word
Module 2	Presentations with PowerPoint®
Module 3	Spreadsheets with Excel
Module 4	Desktop Publishing with Word
Module 5	Integrated Project (Word, Excel, PowerPoint®)
Module 6	Database with Access
Module 7	Desktop Information Management with Outlook
Module 8	Integrated Project (Word, Excel, PowerPoint®, Access, Outlook)
Module 9	Input Technologies
Module 10	Multimedia with Macromedia® Fireworks®
Module 11	Web Page Design with FrontPage®

Text/CD (Modules 1-8)	0-538-72827-2
Text/CD (Modules 1-11)	0-538-72888-4

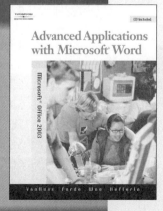

Advanced Applications with Microsoft® Word 2E

Take document processing out of the classroom and into the workplace with this one-of-a-kind text. Users face realistic workplace challenges in UBI, a simulated incubator company. Students integrate business vocabulary, critical thinking, workplace strategies, and Web research skills as they learn more about document processing. Key workplace skills include: communication, ethics, training, leadership, productivity, time management, and customer service.

Text/CD 0-538-72828-0

Contents

Overview of Jobs

Jobs	Word	Excel	Power-Point	Access	Outlook	E-mail/Internet
Project 1: Getting Organized						
1-1 Key business letter and envelope	✓				✓	
1-2 Create AutoCorrect entries	✓					
1-3 Key memo using a template	✓					✓
1-4 Create electronic calendar					✓	
1-5 Create electronic contacts lists					✓	
1-6 Set up AutoDialer					✓	
1-7 Optional Internet activities						✓
Project 2: Researching						
2-1 Prepare budget worksheet		✓				
2-2 Design bar chart		✓				
2-3 Design pie chart		✓				
2-4 Prepare fee schedule worksheets		✓				
2-5 Optional Internet activities	✓					✓
Project 3: Reporting						
3-1 Prepare formal report	✓	✓				
3-2 Prepare appendix	✓					
3-3 Compose letter of transmittal	✓					
3-4 Design title page	✓					✓
3-5 Prepare list of figures	✓					
3-6 Prepare table of contents	✓					
3-7 Create electronic presentation		✓	✓			
3-8 Prepare fax cover sheet; print slides; update contacts list	✓		✓		✓	✓
3-9 Optional Internet activities			✓			✓
Project 4: Managing Routine Tasks						
4-1 Create and sort table	✓					
4-2 Prepare agenda	✓					
4-3 Edit, sort, and query database; create reports				✓		
4-4 Update calendar					✓	✓
4-5 Design directory for intranet	✓				✓	
4-6 Modify a Table	✓					
4-7 Optional Internet activities						✓

Overview of Jobs						
Jobs	Word	Excel	Power-Point	Access	Outlook	E-mail/Internet
Project 5: Planning the Grand Opening						
5-1 Create worksheet		✓				
5-2 Update calendar and contacts list; display map					✓	✓
5-3 Set up electronic folder for Grand Opening (Windows Explorer)						
5-4 Format table	✓					
5-5 Key memo and assemble documents	✓	✓				
5-6 Design electronic presentation		✓	✓			
5-7 Optional Internet activities						✓
Project 6: Designing Publicity Pieces						
6-1 Design invitation	✓					
6-2 Develop article from outline	✓					✓
6-3 Develop strategy for advertising flyer	✓					
6-4 Prepare newsletter	✓	✓				
6-5 Optional Internet activities						✓
Project 7: Communicating						
7-1 Prepare merge letter and envelopes	✓			✓	✓	
7-2 Update and use database				✓		
7-3 Create database				✓		
7-4 Prepare memo and print labels from database	✓			✓		
7-5 Design announcement and print labels from query	✓			✓		
7-6 Develop handouts and labels	✓			✓		✓
7-7 Merge letter with database	✓			✓		
7-8 Optional Internet activity	✓					✓
Project 8: Managing Information						
8-1 Design application form	✓					
8-2 Research topic and prepare presentation			✓			✓
8-3 Manage files (Windows Explorer)						
8-4 Prepare employment announcement for Web	✓					✓
8-5 Compose memo for Web	✓					✓
8-6 Reformat document for Web	✓					✓
8-7 Select standard theme for documents	✓					
8-8 Optional Internet activity						✓

Welcome to The Sports Connection

The Sports Connection, an integrated Microsoft® Office 2003 simulation, requires you to:

- Apply the complete suite of Microsoft Office 2003 products.
- Perform general office functions.
- Prepare a variety of documents integrating multiple software applications.
- Be resourceful in obtaining, organizing, analyzing, evaluating, and managing information.
- Enhance your communication and interpersonal skills.
- Use critical-thinking skills to make effective decisions and solve business problems creatively.
- Work independently, work as a member of an internal team, and work as a member of an external team.
- Be creative as you determine ways to increase productivity by being both more efficient and more effective.

The Sports Connection setting is realistic, challenging, and interesting. Your position in this simulation is assistant director of The Sports Connection. You report directly to Ms. Karen McKay who has just been named director of The Sports Connection. As the assistant director, you are responsible for managing the office, communicating with users and volunteers, and performing the administrative work for the director.

PREREQUISITES

To accomplish the jobs required by your position as assistant director of The Sports Connection, you must have basic knowledge of the following software applications:

- Microsoft Windows
- Microsoft Word
- Microsoft Excel
- Microsoft PowerPoint
- Microsoft Access

In addition, you will learn how to use a variety of software applications and features if you do not already know how to use them, such as:

- Internet
- Microsoft Outlook
- Autodialer
- Charts
- Sound files
- Electronic mail

DESIGN FEATURES TO ENHANCE LEARNING

The Sports Connection incorporates numerous design features that simplify learning and ensure the smooth integration of software applications to accomplish a variety of tasks. You are taught to perform tasks just as they would be performed in a business setting.

- The objectives for each job specify the skills required to perform that job.
- Software Tips aid you in performing less frequently used or specialized functions.
- Specific step-by-step directions are provided to assist you with some advanced or specialized functions of the software.
- A training manual provides basic, step-by-step instructions for Outlook, including Autodialer, that you may not have learned prior to beginning the simulation.
- Internet icons alert you to activities that involve Internet usage; intranet options are also included. The final job in each project provides additional, optional Internet activities designed to help you learn practical uses of the Internet in the performance of typical business tasks.
- Time management, work organization, and teamwork skills are enhanced through the effective use of software applications, such as Outlook, and the track changes features of Microsoft Word.

STANDARDIZED FORMAT AND PROCEDURES

Most businesses and organizations generally adopt a standardized format to promote corporate identity, enhance their image, and improve productivity. The Sports Connection follows this commonly accepted business practice by:

- Providing a logo on disk for use in document preparation.
- Standardizing document formats (i.e., block letter style with open punctuation, Professional template for memos).
- Using electronic mail for all memos if it is available.
- Standardizing office procedures so that directions are not needed (i.e., creating group or user distribution lists for classmates, always updating the calendar when activities affect it).

DATA FILES

To complete the activities in this text, you will use the Data CD-ROM. Your instructor will install the files to *X*:\SportsCon (*X* refers to the drive, folder *SportsCon*). If the CD is packaged in the back of this textbook, you may install the CD-ROM on your own personal computer. The data files will be used to complete the exercises in this text.

INTRODUCTION

The Community Foundation created The Sports Connection as a result of a $5 million donation from an anonymous donor. The sole purpose of the Community Foundation is to foster a better quality of life in the New Orleans community. It is a publicly supported endowment that receives gifts from donors to make grants for local charitable purposes.

Endowments provide a permanent source of income because the money is invested and only the earnings are used. Donors may designate who receives the benefits and the conditions under which the proceeds may be used. Once a grant has been made to an organization, such as The Sports Connection, the Community Foundation must ensure that the expenditure of funds meets the criteria established by the donor. This oversight is accomplished by an established reporting procedure and by

having an *ex officio* member on the governing board, The Sports Connection Advisory Council.

THE SPORTS CONNECTION MISSION

The mission of The Sports Connection is to promote good sportsmanship, fitness, good health, and recreational activities for young people in an environment that enhances good community relations. The Sports Connection especially seeks to ensure that young women and financially disadvantaged young men and women are an integral part of the activities provided by The Sports Connection.

THE SPORTS CONNECTION SITE

The physical facility consists of a converted school that was vacated when schools were consolidated and a park. The vacated school had a gymnasium, a cafeteria, several large classrooms, an office suite, and several large rest rooms. The area of the park designed to appeal to very young children has a play ground with outdoor equipment and a large open area used for organized activities, such as T-ball, soccer, and other sports. The area of the park designed to appeal to teenagers and young adults is near the recreational facility and has a swimming pool, several tennis courts, and several acres of land used for baseball, soccer, and softball.

CRITERIA FOR ESTABLISHING THE SPORTS CONNECTION

The entire donation must be used to enhance the park and recreational facility the donor's father anonymously gave to the city twenty years ago. The appropriate city officials approved the gift and agreed to continue maintaining the park and recreational facility by providing basic maintenance, insurance, utilities, and security. The gift agreement specifies the following criteria:

- Of the $5 million gift, $3 million must be placed in an endowment in the Community Foundation, which will invest the money and distribute 5 percent of the endowment each year to The Sports Connection provided the earnings are adequate to do so. The remainder of the earnings are added to the endowment so that it continues to grow.

- The remaining $2 million is to be used to up-grade and equip the indoor sports facility and the park area and to cover the operational budget for the first year since earnings will not be available during the first year.
- An Advisory Council with diverse representation will oversee the financial and operational activities of The Sports Connection.
- All aspects of The Sports Connection must be available at no charge to young people who are financially disadvantaged (as determined by the Community Foundation guidelines).
- The facilities and activities must be designed to appeal to young women, and the Advisory Council must demonstrate that appropriate resources are allocated to ensure that young women are an integral part of The Sports Connection.
- The Advisory Council should solicit corporate sponsorships, donations, and volunteers to enhance the operations of The Sports Connection.
- Efforts must be made to introduce all youth to sports and activities that are often available only to the more affluent segments of society.
- Educational activities—particularly as they relate to fitness and health—as well as efforts to build good sportsmanship must be an integral part of The Sports Connection.
- Efforts must be made to publicize the opening of The Sports Connection and to make the community aware of the resources it provides for youth.

ACTION PLAN FOR THE SPORTS CONNECTION

Your work as assistant director of The Sports Connection is divided into eight projects. Each project has an introductory page describing your activities for that project. The projects are:

Project 1   Getting Organized
Project 2   Researching
Project 3   Reporting
Project 4   Managing Routine Tasks
Project 5   Planning the Grand Opening
Project 6   Designing Publicity Pieces
Project 7   Communicating
Project 8   Managing Information

Jobs within each project are numbered. Some jobs are further subdivided into two or more tasks.

STANDARD OPERATING PROCEDURES

- Complete the exercises in the Software Training Manual that begins on page 119 before beginning Project 1.
- Create a folder for each project in which to store your solutions. Name the folders *Project 1 Solutions*, *Project 2 Solutions*, etc. Save the solutions for each task in the proper folder.
- Spell-check each document when you complete it. Then proofread the document carefully to check for errors the spell-checker didn't find.
- Use block letter style with open punctuation as the standard format unless specified otherwise.
- Use the Professional Memo template for hard copy memos.
- Use unbound style for reports unless specified otherwise. Use a 2″ top margin for the first page and default side margins throughout. Number the pages.

© GETTY IMAGES/PHOTODISC

scenario

As assistant director of The Sports Connection, you are responsible for preparing routine letters, memos, and envelopes. Use the block letter style with open punctuation for all letters, and, unless specified otherwise, send memos via electronic mail. If electronic mail is not available, follow the steps shown in each job for sending by hard copy.

You are skilled in the numerous features offered by Microsoft Office and are eager to assist the new director in "getting organized." One of the first organizing tasks you will do is to set up Ms. McKay's calendar using Outlook. You will use this desktop information management software to schedule appointments, record tasks, monitor the progress of major tasks, and create and maintain various contact lists.

profile

Getting Organized

project

1

Key Business Letter and Envelope

- Key a business letter with special notations and an envelope
- Use a template
- Use Outlook Contacts data

You will use Outlook to maximize your efficiency in preparing this letter and envelope. Complete the *Contacts* section of the Software Training Manual before completing Job 1-1.

Key a letter from Ms. McKay to Mr. Wallace T. Brooks, Chairperson of the Community Foundation Board of Directors, accepting her appointment as director of The Sports Connection. You will find his address in the Advisory Council folder in Outlook. (Software Training Manual, p. 134.)

In Outlook, select the *New Letter to Contact* feature to create the letter. Using the Letter Wizard, choose Professional Letter for the page design. Assume the letter will be printed on New Orleans Park and Recreation Center letterhead. Begin the letter about 2" from the top of the page. Select a business salutation, subject (*Contract Acceptance*), appropriate complimentary closing, enclosure notation, and copy to the Community Foundation Board of Directors. The letter is from Karen McKay, Director.

When the letter is opened, key the body of the letter from the next page. Format the letter in the acceptable Sports Connection style—block with open punctuation. If time permits, key the company name and address in a letterhead you design at the top of the page.

New Orleans Park and Recreation Center
5600 St. Charles Avenue
New Orleans, LA 70115-8264
(504) 555-0139

Create an envelope for the letter and add it to the document. Omit the return address. Save the file as **Brooks Letter**.

> **Check the Software Training Manual.**

August 18, 20--

Mr. Wallace T. Brooks, Chairperson
Community Foundation Board of Directors
P.O. Box 19039
New Orleans, LA 70115-8239

Dear Mr. Brooks

Contract Acceptance

The recent gift to the City of New Orleans is truly exciting, and I am very pleased to accept your offer to serve as the director of The Sports Connection. Having served as director of the New Orleans Park and Recreation Center for the past six years, I am excited about the opportunities now available to our youth and citizens. I am very eager to continue the current outstanding programs, coordinate the renovation project, and direct a team that will bring us to the forefront of sports facilities offering innovative programs for its citizens.

Mr. Brooks, I commend the Community Foundation for the mission of The Sports Connection <u>to promote good sportsmanship, fitness, good health, and recreational activities for all residents of New Orleans</u>. This gift will take us the distance in making our mission a reality in New Orleans, and I feel fortunate to be a part of this team.

Two signed originals of my employment contract are enclosed. I have retained the third copy for my records.

My staff has completed all preparations for the 2 p.m. press conference on August 30 to announce the donation and the name change from New Orleans Park and Recreation Center to The Sports Connection. You will need to arrive at City Hall at 1:30 p.m.

1-2

Create AutoCorrect Entries

SOFTWARE

AutoCorrect
Tools, AutoCorrect
Options, AutoCorrect
tab

- Create AutoCorrect entries for frequently keyed text

Add the following entries to the AutoCorrect feature of your word processing software. By taking a few minutes now to enter these frequently keyed entries, you will save much time in keying and proofreading later.

Replace	With
sc	*The Sports Connection*
NO	*New Orleans*
cf	*Community Foundation Board of Directors*
GO	*Grand Opening*
km	*Karen McKay, Director*

As you complete the simulation, add other entries as you identify frequently used words or phrases. Keep a list of these entries and submit the completed list to the instructor at the end of the simulation.

Key Memo Using a Template

- Key a memo using a template

- Transmit via e-mail (optional)

Ms. McKay wishes to inform all current employees of New Orleans Park and Recreation Center of the $5 million donation and the name change of the center. This communication must receive priority this morning as the staff is encouraged to attend the 2 p.m. press conference.

Prepare the memo in Word using the Professional memo template. Be sure to:

- Key *New Orleans Park and Recreation Center* as the company name.

- Key *Staff Distribution List* in the **TO** position in the heading.

- Delete the copy notation in the memo heading.

- Make the corrections as indicated. See the Software Tip for help with inserting the em dashes in the last paragraph.

- Save the file as **Donation Memo**.

NOTE

The em dash is a symbol—once only available to typesetters—that denotes the dash and indicates a long pause.

SOFTWARE

Em Dash
Insert menu, Symbols, Special Characters tab

If e-mail technology is available:
In your e-mail software, create a group list (distribution list) that includes the members of your class. Name the group *Park Staff*. In the memo in Word, click the *E-mail* button on the Standard toolbar. Enter or select the Park Staff distribution list you created in the **To** field. Enter an appropriate subject line. Send the message.

If e-mail technology is not available:
At the bottom of the memo below the reference initials, list the names of five of your class members after *Distribution List*. List the names horizontally so that the memo remains a one-page document.

(Cont. on next page)

1-3

FROM: Karen McKay, Director
DATE: August 19, 20--
SUBJECT: $5 Million Donation to Be Announced

Coming to the city this month as an anonymous gift,
We are pleased to announce to our staff the receipt of a
$5 million gift to the New Orleans Park and Recreation Center.
The major intent of this generous gift is to:

1. Provide an endowment fund of $3 million *sp.* to the Community
   Foundation. Specifications allow 5% of the earnings to be
   distributed to the New Orleans Park and Recreation Center
   each year (provided earnings are adequate).

2. Provide $2 million to the New Orleans Park and Recreation *and the park area*
   Center to update and equip an indoor sports facility and to
   fund the operational budget for the first year.

4. Design sports and fitness programs that will help all youth.

5. Plan educational programs that will teach young people *to build good sportsmanship and* to
   develop a positive attitude toward fitness and health.

3. Establish an advisory council to oversee the financial and
   operational activities.

The opportunities that this donation offers our center
~~particularly young women~~ and the ~~disadvantaged~~ youth of New
Orleans are tremendous. Your commitment to your position is
greatly appreciated, and your continued contributions and
commitment are very much needed as we all work together this
next year to plan The Sports Connection. *bold*

That's right The Sports Connection a new name and a new
direction for the youth and citizens of New Orleans. You are
all invited to attend the official announcement that will be
made today at a 2:00 p.m. press conference at City Hall. I
look forward to seeing many of you there.

1-4

Create Electronic Calendar

- Learn to use Outlook software
- Schedule appointments
- Enter tasks and print calendar

One of your responsibilities is to maintain Ms. McKay's calendar. This involves scheduling appointments, canceling and rescheduling appointments, and posting items to the Task List. You also print copies of the Calendar daily.

You will use Outlook, known as a desktop organizer or PIM (personal information manager), to complete these duties. Complete the Software Training Manual before completing this job.

> **Check the Software Training Manual.**

1-4

ENTER APPOINTMENTS

Make the following entries for Ms. McKay using the Calendar feature. Set each label as *Business*.

August 20	*Meeting with Stan Williams, Ms. McKay's office, 8:30 a.m. Allow 30 minutes for this appointment.*
September 6	*Meeting with Javier Ortega, architect, and C. Rebecca Hunter, structural engineer, at Ortega's office (389 Wilbrook Street), 10 a.m. Allow two hours.*
September 6	*Meeting with Community Foundation (CF) Executive Committee, Conference Room, 3 p.m. Allow two hours. Add note to have coffee and cookies delivered at 2:45.*
September 7	*Meeting with Joyce Smith every week on this day of the week, Ms. McKay's office, 11 a.m. Allow one hour. Make recurring meeting.*
September 8	*Meeting with Sports Program Leaders, Conference Room, 1 p.m. Allow one hour. Make recurring meeting. Attach the file **Agenda 9-8**.*
September 8	*Meeting with James Cleveland, Athletics Director, and Barbara Thrasher, Senior Women's Administrator, Central University Athletics Department, in Ms. McKay's office, 9 a.m. Allow $1^1/_2$ hours.*

Agenda 9-8

(Cont. on next page)

8

Project 1

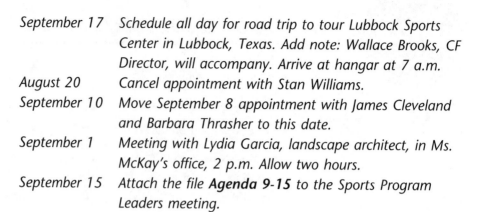

September 17   *Schedule all day for road trip to tour Lubbock Sports Center in Lubbock, Texas. Add note: Wallace Brooks, CF Director, will accompany. Arrive at hangar at 7 a.m.*

August 20   *Cancel appointment with Stan Williams.*

September 10   *Move September 8 appointment with James Cleveland and Barbara Thrasher to this date.*

September 1   *Meeting with Lydia Garcia, landscape architect, in Ms. McKay's office, 2 p.m. Allow two hours.*

September 15   *Attach the file Agenda 9-15 to the Sports Program Leaders meeting.*

Agenda 9-15

ENTER TASKS

Another effective time management procedure is entering tasks to be completed and prioritizing those tasks. Make the following task entries for Ms. McKay using the Calendar feature.

Task 1: Formal Report and Presentation to Community Foundation Board of Directors

The start date is September 1 of the current year and the due date is September 20 of the current year. Make high priority. Mark it 25% complete.

Set status as *In Progress.*

Add the following notes:

Work with accountant on cost projections.
Develop new fee schedule.
Conduct research on innovative activities in sports centers today.
Develop formal report.
Develop PowerPoint presentation.

Insert the file **Current Fee Schedule**.

Current Schedule Fee

Task 2: Plan Grand Opening

The start date is January 4 of next year and the due date is February 4 of next year. Make high priority. Mark it 10% complete.

Set status as *In Progress.*

Add the following notes:

Publicity Pieces
    Invitation
    Newspaper article
    Newsletter

8

Mailouts to Various Databases
Program
Decorations
Follow up

Planning Notes for
Grand Opening

Insert the file **Planning Notes for Grand Opening**.

PRINT CALENDAR

Prepare a footer that will print at the bottom of Ms. McKay's calendar to include her name, the page number, and the date printed. Print Ms. McKay's calendar in

1. daily style (1 page/day) for September 15

2. tri-fold style for each day September 6-10 (Ms. McKay keeps this in her briefcase.)

1-5

Create Electronic Contacts Lists

- Create electronic folders for new contacts

- Enter information for contacts

You realize the value of a comprehensive and well-maintained contacts list. Creating folders for each type of contact is critical. Entering information on new contacts and consistently inputting updates to the contacts list are important tasks to be completed as the assistant director. You also take advantage of the automatic phone dialing feature when placing calls to these contacts.

ENTER CONTACTS

Task 1

Create a folder labeled *General Contacts*. Place the new folder in the Contacts folder. Add the following new contacts.

Full Name	Mr. James Cleveland	Dr. Barbara Thrasher	Ms. Lydia Garcia	Mr. Javier Ortega
Job Title	Athletics Director	Senior Women's Administrator	Landscape Architect	Architect
Company	Central University	Central University	Simmons Landscape Company	Ortega-Hunter Architects, PA
Business Address	23 Easton Boulevard New Orleans, LA 70115-0023	23 Easton Boulevard New Orleans, LA 70115-0023	P.O. Box 3893 New Orleans, LA 70115-3893	1433 North Elm Street New Orleans, LA 70115-1433
Business Phone	(504) 555-0103	(504) 555-0113	(504) 555-0176	(504) 555-0153
Home Phone				
Mobile Phone	(504) 555-0114	(504) 555-0143	(504) 555-0158	(504) 555-0171
Business Fax	(504) 555-0134	(504) 555-0134	(504) 555-0142	(504) 555-0193
E-mail	Jcleveland@central.edu	Bthrasher@central.edu		
Web Page Address	http://www.communityfoundation.org	http://www.central.edu/thrasher		

Task 2

Create a new Contacts folder called *CF Directors* for the Community Foundation Board of Directors. Add the following new contacts.

Full Name	Mr. Wallace T. Brooks	Ms. Lisa Mostella	Ms. Doris Ondracek	Mr. Thomas Fairdixon	Mr. Raymond Woo
Job Title	Chairperson				
Company	Community Foundation Board of Directors	Community Foundation Board of Directors	Community Foundation Board of Directors	Community Foundation Board of Directors	Community Foundation Board of Directors
Business Address	P.O. Box 19039 New Orleans, LA 70115-8329	23 Main Street New Orleans, LA 70115-0023	100 Fourth St. New Orleans, LA 70115-0100	110 Board Ave. New Orleans, LA 70115-0110	631 Pinkerton St. New Orleans, LA 70115-0631
Business Phone	(504) 555-0139	(504) 555-0187	(504) 555-0194	(504) 555-0189	(504) 555-0192
Home Phone	(504) 555-0109	(504) 555-0197	(504) 555-0148	(504) 555-0164	(504) 555-0100
Mobile Phone	(504) 555-0155	(504) 555-0180	(504) 555-0125	(504) 555-0162	(504) 555-0183
Business Fax	(504) 555-0129	(504) 555-0101	(504) 555-0132	(504) 555-0166	(504) 555-0122
E-mail	Wbrooks@cf.org	Lmostella@cf.org	Dondracek@cf.org	Tfairdixon@cf.org	Rwoo@cf.org

Task 3: Advisory Council

If you completed the Software Training Manual, you have already created a folder for listing potential members of the Advisory Council to be appointed next month. (If you have not done so, create this folder.) This Advisory Council will meet monthly to offer relevant advice in the planning of The Sports Connection.

Add six new contacts that you select from your local area. Select the contacts carefully using the following information:

1. Corporate executive

2. University professor

3. Physician with interest in sports medicine

4. Sports professional (coach, athletic director, league board member, etc.)

5. Accountant

6. Other (select someone who could contribute to an Advisory Council for The Sports Connection)

Task 4: Print Contact Lists

Print the three Contacts lists using Card Style. Use the default option that prints contacts immediately after each other. On the Page Setup dialog box, choose *None* for the *Blank forms at end* option. Update the footer to include Karen McKay's name.

1-6

Set Up AutoDialer

- Learn to use AutoDialer

- Set up calls using AutoDialer

The selection of the Advisory Council is complete, and Ms. McKay has chosen to call each nominee and invite him or her personally to serve on the Advisory Council. She asks you to initiate the next call as soon as she finishes with the previous call.

Use the AutoDialer feature to call a physician, corporate executive, and university educator. If your system is not connected to a modem, the call cannot be connected. Just follow the steps up to the point of clicking *Start Call*.

> **Check the Software Training Manual for AutoDialer.**

CRITICAL THINKING

PDAs

MS. MCKAY is considering purchasing a PDA. A PDA (personal digital assistant) is a handheld computer. It runs programs, such as Calendar, Notes, and Contacts, like those found in Microsoft Outlook. Versions of other programs, such as Word and Excel, are also available for PDAs. Currently, Ms. McKay places a printed copy of her calendar in her briefcase each day so she can see her appointments when she is away from the office. If she had a PDA, the information would be available electronically. By completing a simple process called *synchronization*, appointments, contacts, tasks, and other information can be updated from a PC to a PDA or from a PDA to a PC.

1. What advantages might Ms. McKay find when using a PDA?
2. What disadvantages might Ms. McKay find when using a PDA?
3. Would you recommend that Ms. McKay purchase a PDA? Give reasons for your recommendation.

The Start menu on a Pocket PC PDA provides access to programs and features.

1-7

Optional Internet Activities: IRS

- Download tax form from Internet

- Locate address on Internet

It is time to file your individual tax return. You need a copy of the current Form 1040 U.S. Individual Income Tax Return. Having just moved to New Orleans, you do not know where to file your return.

URL: http://www.irs.ustreas.gov/

Task 1: Download and Print File

1. Create a new folder on the hard drive; name it *Download*.

2. Go to **http://www.irs.ustreas.gov/**. Click *Forms and Publications*. Under *Download forms and publications by*, click *Form and Instruction Number*. Choose *PDF* as the file format.

3. Scroll the list of forms and select the most recent Form 1040 U.S. Individual Income Tax Return. Click *Review Selected Files*. Click the link for the form name. The form will open in the browser window.

4. Click the *Save* button on the Acrobat toolbar. Save the form as **f1040.pdf**. Print the form.

Task 2: Find IRS Mailing Address

Follow the same procedures as in Task 1 to find and save the general instructions for completing Form 1040 U.S. Individual Income Tax Return. From this document, find the address for mailing the completed Form 1040 for Ms. McKay, who lives in New Orleans.

Note

If necessary, download Adobe Acrobat or a similar program to view and navigate or print the PDF file.

© GETTY IMAGES/PHOTODISC

scenario

Research skills have always been essential for the competitive organization. Similarly, today with instant access to information via the Internet, managers and their assistants must be astute at using search engines to locate information that will sell their products; persuade a buyer, board member, etc.; or provide insight into issues. Because of your Internet skills and your interest in research, Ms. McKay often asks you to compile information related to various topics.

In addition to Internet research, organizations need financial worksheets and charts that can be used to convince an audience, present information, and show integrity. In this project, you will create two worksheets and two charts that will be used in both a written report and a slide presentation to the Community Foundation Board of Directors.

profile

Researching

project

2

Prepare Budget Worksheet

- Key worksheet, entering formulas for subtotals and totals

- Format worksheet using fonts, shading, footer, and borders

1. Enter the budget worksheet shown on pages 17 and 18. Leave Rows 3 and 55 blank as shown.

2. Enter formulas where indicated that use the SUM function to total each category and to total all the categories. For example, in Cell C15, the formula would be =SUM(B5:B15). Format the numbers to display 0 decimals.

3. Format the main title in Row 1 for Arial, 12-point font. Format all other cells for Arial, 10-point font (the default).

4. In Rows 1 and 2, center the worksheet titles across Columns A through C.

5. Apply bold to the main title in Row 1, the ten budget categories, and **Subtotal** each time it appears. Make **Total Budget** in Row 56 bold also. (*Hint:* Hold down the *Ctrl* key and click cells to select several of them. Then click the *Bold* button.)

6. Indent expenses within categories one level. (Select cells and click the *Increase Indent* button to create a Left Indent 1.) Indent **Subtotal** two levels each time it appears.

7. Format Cells B5, C15, and C56 as currency. (*Hint:* Choose *Format, Cells*. On the *Number* tab, choose *Currency, 0* decimal places, and the $ symbol.) Format all numbers for 0 decimal places.

8. Select Cells A1:C2 and apply a single line top and bottom border. Select cells A56:C56 (the Total row.) Apply a single line top border and a double line bottom border.

9. Apply a single line bottom border to the following ranges:
   B14:C14
   B20:C20
   B27:C27
   B34:C34
   B38:C38
   B45:C45
   B50:C50

(Cont. on page 18)

2-1

	A	B	C	D
1	**The Sports Connection Budget**			
2	Fiscal Year 7/1/20-- through 6/30/20--			
3				
4	**Building Renovations**			
5	Painting, repairs, interior construction work	$250,000		
6	Reconfigure to have 2 basketball courts, 1 volleyball court	150,000		
7	Convert 2 classrooms to aerobic center	25,000		
8	Convert 2 classrooms and 2 rest rooms to locker rooms	150,000		
9	Convert 1 classroom to a seminar/conference room	25,000		
10	Convert section of cafeteria to staff lounge and user lounge	50,000		
11	Improve handicap access	50,000		
12	Reconfigure office area	10,000		
13	Convert remaining cafeteria section to fitness center	50,000		
14	Reserve for contingencies	40,000		
15	Subtotal		Formula	
16	**General Park Upgrade**			
17	Add walking, jogging, and bike trails	30,000		
18	Upgrade playground area	20,000		
19	Improve lighting and landscaping	50,000		
20	Add picnic and shelter areas	50,000		
21	Subtotal		Formula	
22	**Playing Field Area Upgrade**			
23	Improve lighting	75,000		
24	Add bleacher sections	25,000		
25	Improve drainage and hydro-seed to improve turf	50,000		
26	Add fencing behind batting area and in needed areas	50,000		
27	Lay out soccer, baseball, and softball fields	50,000		
28	Subtotal		Formula	
29	**Swimming Pool and Tennis Court Upgrades**			
30	Resurface tennis courts	75,000		
31	Repair fence and upgrade area surrounding tennis courts	25,000		
32	Improve lighting	25,000		
33	Resurface pool deck	25,000		
34	Repair fence and upgrade area surrounding pool	25,000		
35	Subtotal		Formula	
36	**Driving Range and Practice Putting Green Construction**			
37	Driving range	40,000		
38	Practice putting green	45,000		
39	Subtotal		Formula	

(Cont. on page 18)

10. Select Cells A1:C2 and apply light green shading. Select cells A56:C56 and apply light green shading.

11. Change the row height to **20** for Rows 16, 22, 29, 36, 40, 47, 52, 53, and 54. This will add space between the categories and make the worksheet easier to read.

12. The default name for the worksheet is *Sheet1*. Rename the worksheet as **Budget**. (*Hint:* Right-click the worksheet tab and choose *Rename*.)

SOFTWARE

Excel Custom Footer
View menu, Header and Footer, Custom Footer

13. Create a custom footer for the worksheet. In the left position, key *Prepared by Karen McKay*. In the center position, key *Page* and insert the page number. (Click the *Number* button on the Header/Footer toolbar.) In the right position, insert the date. (Click the *Date* button on the Header/Footer toolbar.)

14. Access the Page Setup dialog box. On the Margins tab, select *Horizontally* and *Vertically* to center the worksheet on the page. On the Page tab, click the *Fit to* radio button. Enter **1** for pages wide and **1** for tall to scale the worksheet to print on one page.

15. Use Print Preview to check the format of the worksheet. The budget total should be $2,000,000. When the sheet is correct, print the worksheet. Save the worksheet as **Budget**.

(Cont. from page 17)

2-1

	A B		C	D
40	**Equipment and Furniture**			
41	Fitness equipment	100,000		
42	Sports equipment	75,000		
43	Office furniture and equipment	35,000		
44	Seminar room furniture and equipment	15,000		
45	Furniture for staff/volunteer and user lounges	25,000		
46	**Subtotal**		Formula	
47	**Grand Opening**			
48	Printing, decorations, and publicity	10,000		
49	Picnic in park on opening day	25,000		
50	Reserve for contingencies	5,000		
51	**Subtotal**		Formula	
52	**Architect and Professional Fees**		50,000	
53	**Operational Budget for First Year (= to 5% of endowment)**		150,000	
54	**Reserve for Contingencies**		50,000	
55				
56	**Total Budget**		Formula	
57				

2-2

Design Bar Chart

- Create bar chart from worksheet

- Format bar chart

S O F T W A R E

Hold down the *Ctrl* key to select several nonadjacent cells.

1. Open the **Budget** Excel file created in 2-1. You will prepare a bar chart comparing the ten budget categories.

2. Rename Sheet2 as *Bar Chart Data.* On the Budget sheet, select the ten cells that hold the names of the budget categories (Building Renovations, General Park Upgrade, etc.). Click the *Copy* button on the Standard toolbar. Go to the Bar Chart Data sheet, Cell A1, and click the *Paste* button on the Standard toolbar. The ten categories should now appear in A1:A10.

3. In Cell B1, enter a formula to display the total for the first category, Building Renovations. To create the formula, click Cell B1. Key =. Click the *Budget* sheet tab. Click Cell C15 that displays the total for the category. Tap *Enter.* The amount should now display on the Bar Chart Data sheet. Repeat this process for the other nine categories.

4. To create a bar chart, select Cells A1:B10 on the Bar Chart Data sheet. Click the *Chart Wizard* button on the Standard toolbar. Select the *Bar* chart type and first chart sub-type.

5. Key *The Sports Connection Budget Category Totals* for the chart title. Choose not to display a legend. Place the chart on a new sheet named *Bar Chart.*

6. Format X-axis data and the values plotted on the Y-axis as follows:
   - Point to chart area and drag to the right until numbers on X-axis appear on one line (only if needed).
   - For the X-axis, change the font to 11 point, dark blue.
   - For the Y-axis, change the font color to dark blue. Change the number format to *Currency* with the $ symbol and 0 decimal places.

7. Format chart title as follows:
   - Change the font to 14 point, dark blue.
   - Insert a hard return after *Budget* to make the title appear on two lines if needed.

8. Change the color of the chart plot area to light yellow. Change the color of bars to blue.

9. Save the workbook using the same name. Print the Bar Chart sheet.

2-2

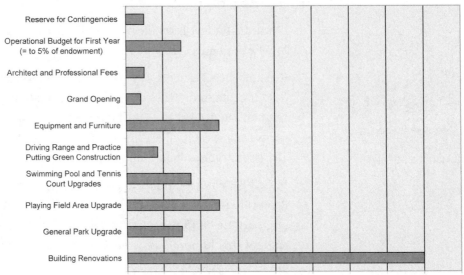

**The Sports Connection Budget
Category Totals**

2-3

Design Pie Chart

- Create pie chart showing projected costs

- Format pie chart

1. Open the **Budget** Excel file created in 2-2. Go to the Budget sheet.

2. Create a pie chart with 3-D visual effects showing the breakdown of Grand Opening category.

3. Key *Grand Opening Expenditures* for the title. Do not show a legend. For data labels, display the category names and percentages.

4. Place the chart on a new sheet named *Pie Chart*.

5. Format chart title and data labels as follows:
   - For the labels, change the font to 16 point, dark blue.
   - For the chart title, change the font to 26 point, dark blue.

6. Change chart background to yellow.

7. If desired, change the color of the pie slices. Be aware of how colors relate to the background and to each other. If time permits, search the Internet for research on color.

8. Save the worksheet using the same name. Print the chart.

Optional: Create charts for other budget categories to show breakdown of costs.

2-3

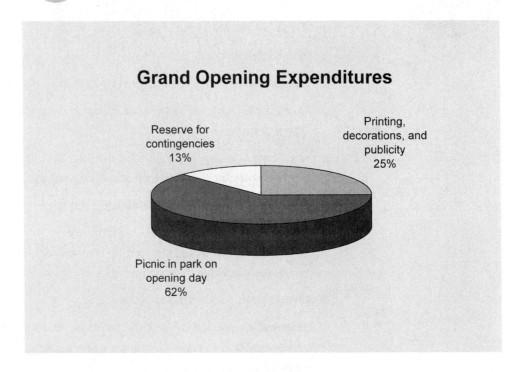

Grand Opening Expenditures

Reserve for
contingencies
13%

Printing,
decorations, and
publicity
25%

Picnic in park on
opening day
62%

CRITICALTHINKING

Charts

CHARTS CAN be an important part of a report or presentation. Because charts present information graphically, readers may be able to grasp comparisons of data more quickly by looking at a chart than by reading a table of numbers. Showing the correct information in a chart in a way that is not misleading is very important.

1. You have been given the information below to present in chart format. What type of chart should you use to compare the individual expenses to the total amount?
2. What is wrong with the data for the chart? Would this issue be apparent when the data is graphed in the type of chart you indicated for question 1? Why or why not? How would the error affect the appearance of the chart?

Food by Day

Monday	$57.00	Airfare	$289.67
Tuesday	$45.50	Rental car	$193.59
Wednesday	$35.75	Hotel	$765.45
Thursday	$42.50	Total Food	$226.25
		Meeting registration	$150.00
		Total Expenses	$1,624.96

2-4

Prepare Fee Schedule Worksheets

- Prepare fee schedule worksheets

- Format worksheets with color and borders

1. In a new workbook, key the fee schedules on two separate sheets as shown. Rename Sheet 1 as *Passes*. Rename Sheet 2 as *Other Programs*.

2. Format the amounts in Column B as Currency with the $ symbol and two decimal places. (Choose *Format, Cells, Currency*. The $ sign will appear next to the number using this command.)

3. On the Other Programs sheet, add other programs that would be appropriate for The Sports Connection to offer. Be sure to include a fee for each one.

4. Format the worksheet titles and use the same font sizes as for the Budget worksheet created in Job 2-1. Change the row height to 20 for the rows that contain the category names (except the first one that follows a blank row).

5. Create a custom footer for both worksheets as you did for the Budget worksheet. For both worksheets, set the top margin to 1" and center the worksheet horizontally on the page. Save the workbook as **Fee Schedule**.

2-4

Sheet 1

The Sports Connection	
Fee Schedule for Passes	

Blank row →

Weekly Passes	Fee
Full access (no charge)	$0.00
Full access	$25.00
Fitness Center only	$15.00
Pool only	$12.00
Locker facilities	$8.00
Monthly Passes	**Fee**
Full access (no charge)	$0.00
Full access	$60.00
Fitness Center only	$40.00
Pool only	$30.00
Locker facilities	$20.00
Daily Passes	**Fee**
Pool	$5.00
Fitness Center	$10.00
Locker facilities	$2.00

Blank row →

(Cont. on page 24)

Sheet 2

Blank row ⟶

The Sports Connection	
Fee Schedule for Other Programs	
Special Services	**Fees**
Driving range	
Small bucket of balls	$3.50
Big bucket of balls	$5.00
Putting green (per quarter hour)	$3.00
Batting cage (per 25 balls)	$2.50
Day Care Facility Fees	
Hourly	$5.00
After School Program (5)	$25.00
Special Programming*	**Weekly Fees**
Aerobics Classes	
Beginning Aerobics (3)	$15.00
Intermediate Aerobics (3)	$15.00
Water Aerobics for Children (3)	$15.00
Water Aerobics for Youth (3)	$15.00
Water Aerobics for Adults (3)	$15.00
Strength Training (2)	$10.00
Flexibility Class for Seniors (3)	$15.00
Fitness for Life Classes (2)	
Ages 10-12	$10.00
Ages 13-15	$10.00
Ages 16-18	$10.00
Sportsmanship 101	
Ages 8-10	$10.00
Ages 11-14	$10.00
Ages 15-18	$10.00
Swimming Classes	
Beginning Swimming (5)	$25.00
Intermediate Swimming (5)	$25.00
Advanced Swimming (5)	$25.00
Golf Lessons	
Beginning Golf (2)	$35.00
Intermediate Golf (2)	$35.00

Blank row ⟶

* Number of meetings per week shown in parentheses.

Blank row ⟶

2-5 Optional Internet Activities: Research Speech

- Choose one of three speech topics

- Research the topic using the Internet and other resources

- Compose an outline of the speech

- Compile research in a useful format

Ms. McKay has been invited to speak for several civic and professional organizations, including the Chamber of Commerce Annual Banquet and the Central University Physical Education Association Initiation Ceremony. She has asked you to compile information from the Internet and other local resources for the following speaking engagements.

Topic	Organization	Date
Youth Fitness and Exercise	Central University Physical Education Association	September 20
Youth Nutrition	Association of Parents and Teachers	October 5
Youth Fitness Programs/Campaigns	Chamber of Commerce	November 23

1. Choose **one** of the speech topics listed above.

2. Identify key words for use in Internet search engines. Key words may include but are not limited to: teen nutrition, youth fitness, exercise, youth fitness programs.

3. Locate and save or print six articles pertaining to the speech topic.

4. Write an outline for the speech.

5. Compile pertinent information in a format that will be useful to Ms. McKay as she composes each section of the speech. Be sure to include documentation for the source and include the URL if located on the Internet.

Optional:

1. Contact local organizations and use local directories to locate information.

2. Use the Internet to contact your local public library for books and other reference materials.

© GETTY IMAGES/PHOTODISC

scenario

The budget for The Sports Connection has been developed. Now a formal written report is being prepared for distribution to the Community Foundation Board of Directors. Because it is a formal report, a creative title page, letter of transmittal, table of contents, and list of figures are required. In this case, the full budget will be included in the appendix as well as a pie chart that will clarify the breakdown of expenditures for the grand opening event.

Finally, you will prepare PowerPoint slides for the oral presentation Ms. McKay will present to the Community Foundation Board of Directors on October 12.

profile

Reporting

project

3

3-1

Prepare Formal Report

Report

- Key the body of the report

- Embed and edit portions of a worksheet

- Format report headings

- Add figure captions

The first step in preparing the formal report is to key the actual report itself. Follow
these steps:

1. Open **Report** from the data files. Save as **Budget Report**.
    a. Begin the first page at approximately 2″ from the top.
    b. Set the left margin at 1.5″ and the right margin at 1″. DS (double-space) the
        report.
    c. Center the report title in a 16-point, bold, Arial font.
    d. Apply Heading 1 style to the report side headings. (*Hint:* Select the side head-
        ing *Budget*. Click the down arrow for *Style* on the Formatting toolbar. Select
        Heading 1.) Use the Format Painter to apply the Heading 1 style to the other
        side headings.
    e. Apply Heading 2 style to the first paragraph heading in the report. Change
        the font size for the heading to 12 point after applying the style. Use the For-
        mat Painter to apply this modified heading style to the other paragraph head-
        ings in the report.
    f. Insert page numbers to appear at the top right of each page. Do not print a
        page number on page 1.

2. Key the remainder of the report shown on pages 31–32. (Do not prepare figures
    until Step 3.) Apply headings styles to this part of the report.

3. Prepare Figure 1 as an embedded object from the Excel worksheet **Budget** that
    you created in Job 2-1. Follow these steps to insert Figure 1:
    a. Position the insertion point at the end of the paragraph that refers to Figure
        1. Press *Enter*. Position the insertion point in the new blank line.
    b. Open the Excel file **Budget**. Select *A4:C15* (the Building Renovations section).
    c. Click the *Copy* button.
    d. Go to the Word report. The insertion point is already positioned a DS below
        the paragraph where Figure 1 is to be inserted.
    e. Click *Edit* and choose *Paste Special*. The Paste Special dialog box displays as
        shown on the following page.
    f. Click *Paste* and select *Microsoft Excel Worksheet Object*. Click *OK*.

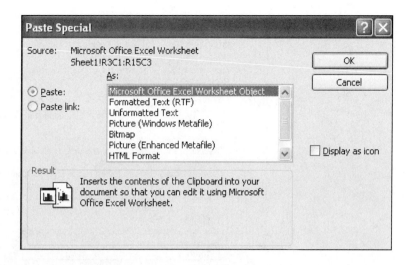

4. Follow these steps to edit the object for Figure 1:

   a. Click the worksheet object to select it; then double-click to edit it. The row and column headings will display when an object is selected for editing.

   b. Insert a new blank row after the *Building Renovations* row.

   c. Select Columns A:C in the Building Renovations row. Click the *Borders* button on the Formatting toolbar and apply *Top and Bottom Border*. Center *Building Renovations* across Columns A:C.

   d. Change *Subtotal* to *Total*. Select A:C in the Total row and apply a *Bottom Border*. Click outside the worksheet to move out of worksheet editing.

5. Add a caption for the figure.

   a. Click the worksheet object once to select it.

   b. Choose *Insert, Reference, Caption*.

   c. After *Figure 1* in the Caption text box, key *Building Renovations*.

   d. Choose to have the caption appear above the figure. Click *OK*.

   e. Leave one single-spaced blank line between the caption and the figure. Figure 1 should display as shown on the following page.

6. Repeat Steps 3 and 4 for embedding and editing Figures 2–7. Format the first amount and the total amount in each figure for currency to match Figure 1. Repeat Step 5 to add a caption to each figure.

7. Repeat Step 3 to insert Figure 8 (Excel file **Fee Schedule**, Passes sheet tab).

   a. Delete the text in Row 1 (The Sports Connection).

   b. Apply *Top and Bottom Border* to the title row.

   c. Format the title for bold. It should be centered across the columns.

   d. Repeat Step 5 to add a caption to the figure.

space from the local schools after consolidation. This space included a gymnasium,

cafeteria, office suite, several large classrooms, and restrooms.

Figure 1 Building Renovations

Building Renovations	
Painting, repairs, interior construction work	$250,000
Reconfigure to have 2 basketball courts, 1 volleyball court	150,000
Convert 2 classrooms to aerobic center	25,000
Convert 2 classrooms and 2 rest rooms to locker rooms	150,000
Convert 1 classroom to a seminar/conference room	25,000
Convert section of cafeteria to staff lounge and user lounge	50,000
Improve handicap access	50,000
Reconfigure office area	10,000
Convert remaining cafeteria section to fitness center	50,000
Reserve for contingencies	40,000
Total	**$800,000**

The largest item in this category is $250,000 designated for painting, repairs, and

some interior construction. Also, adding two basketball courts and one volleyball court;

8. Insert Figure 9 (Excel file **Fee Schedule**, Other Programs sheet tab). The length of the worksheet may require a full page. Follow these steps:

   a. Copy the worksheet in Excel.

   b. Position the insertion point in the report on the page after the last reference in the text to Figure 9.

   c. Insert a manual page break if the sheet requires a full page.

   d. Finish the command to insert the worksheet.

   e. Delete text in Row 1 (The Sports Connection).

   f. Apply *Top and Bottom Border* to the title row.

   g. Format the title for bold. It should be centered across the columns.

   h. Repeat Step 5 to add a caption to the figure.

9. Preview the report using the Print Preview feature.

   a. Note pages where the bottom margin is noticeably more than 1″ because embedded objects were too large to display.

   b. Select the paragraph below the object. Click the *Cut* button.

   c. Move the insertion point to the appropriate location and click the *Paste* button. Repeat as needed to fill the page.

3-1

Fee Schedule

The cost accountants along with the director of The Sports Connection present the fee schedule for your review. The fee schedule consists of two parts: (1) Passes and (2) Other Programs.

Passes. Citizens may purchase weekly, monthly, or daily passes. Weekly and monthly passes include full access to all programs offered by The Sports Connection or only access to the Fitness Center or only the pool. Fees can also be paid to reserve a locker for one's private use only. A no-charge full access pass is also available to citizens meeting the criteria established by the grant specifications. Citizens are asked to complete an application form that will be reviewed by the advisory council. If approved, these individuals will receive a pass for full access at no charge to the individual. Figure 8 outlines the fees for each type of pass. [Insert Figure 8]

Other programs. Additional revenue is also generated from the assessment of special fees for the driving range, putting green, and batting cage. Figure 9 outlines these programs. Also note that rates are based on the number of balls and/or the amount of time in the area. In addition, to accommodate the number of dual working parents, The Sports Connection offers a day care facility for parents using the fitness facility. Fees are based on (1) hourly rates or (2) an after-school package that includes fitness programs for the children in child care.

To fully meet the grant specifications, comprehensive educational programming is required. For this reason, a fee schedule was developed to generate revenue from classes that would require a licensed instructor. Users will be asked to complete surveys, and additional courses will be added accordingly. Figure 9 outlines the specific fees for these programs. Again, citizens who meet the criteria of the grant may complete a special application to waive fees for these programs. [Insert Figure 9 as separate page]

Sponsorships

Two major organizations have joined The Sports Connection and the Community Foundation in their efforts to promote fitness, good health, and recreational activities for young people — Central University Athletic Department and First Bank. [Insert em dash]

(Cont. on next page)

Second

~~First~~, the Board of Directors of First Bank has offered to sponsor a Fun Run on the morning of the grand opening of The Sports Connection. Their staff will design tee-shirts for all participants who sign up ~~to run~~ *for* the various races. Free monthly passes to The Sports Connection will be given to ⑩ *sp* lucky winners. First Bank has indicated a desire to continue the Fun Run each year and designate the proceeds to a scholarship fund for youth desiring to participate ~~on~~ *in* one of the team sports.

First

~~Second~~, the athletic director at Central University proposed a partnership with The Sports Connection and the university to promote interest in girls' soccer, tennis, and volleyball. The plan includes university coaching staff providing educational programming and team coaching for these three areas. The Sports Connection staff will coordinate the registration and class meetings, *will* provides the appropriate equipment, *will* schedules playing fields, and *will* sets up the game/match schedules.

Recommendations

The director of The Sports Connection recommends the approval of the budget set forth in this report with the accompanying justification. The oral report is scheduled for October 12, 200-, at 7 p.m. at the monthly meeting of the Community Foundation Board of Directors. Questions and/or suggestions will be welcomed at this time.

3-2

Prepare Appendix

- Prepare appendices
- Insert bookmarks
- Insert hyperlinks

1. Open the **Budget Report** Word file. Go the end of the report and insert a manual page break.

2. Prepare a title page for Appendix A.
   a. Key *APPENDIX A* at about 2″ from the top. Apply Heading Style 1 and then center the line.
   b. Double space and key *Budget*. Apply the modified Heading Style 2 (12-point) and then center the line.
   c. Add any other design feature you wish to this page, such as a heavy underline, border, or clip art. Use your creativity to create a design.

3. Insert a manual page break. Open the Excel file **Budget** that you created earlier.

4. Use the Copy and Paste Special commands to embed the data from the Budget sheet. In the Word report, click the object to select it. Drag a corner handle to resize the object to fit on one page. Center the object horizontally.

5. Insert another manual page break below the budget. Create a title page for *APPENDIX B Grand Opening Expenditures*. Be consistent with the design created for Appendix A.

6. In the **Budget** file, go to the Pie Chart page. Select and copy the chart. In the Word document, click *Edit, Paste Special*. Choose *Picture (Windows Metafile)*. Click *OK*.

7. Create two bookmarks.
   a. Select the caption *Figure 8, Fee Schedule for Passes* and insert a bookmark named **feeschedule**.
   b. Select *Budget* in the Appendix A title page; insert a bookmark named **budget**.

8. In the second paragraph on page 1 of the report, insert hyperlinks to the *budget* bookmark, the *feeschedule* bookmark, the *Sponsorships* report heading, and the *Recommendations* report heading. (*Hint:* Select the word *budget*; insert a hyperlink; choose the *budget* bookmark. Repeat for other links, choosing the appropriate bookmark or report headings.)

9. Save the file using the same name.

3-3 Compose Letter of Transmittal

- Insert a section break

- Insert a file

- Compose a letter of transmittal

The letter of transmittal is considered a preliminary part of a formal report and is placed at the beginning of the report after the title page. The purposes of the letter of transmittal are (1) to transmit or send the report to the appropriate person or body and (2) to provide important information to the reader(s) that will be helpful in understanding the report.

Key the letter for Ms. McKay's signature. Use the standard format of The Sports Connection.

Letterhead

1. Open the **Budget Report** Word file. Insert a *Next page* section break above the main heading of the report.

2. At the top of the page, insert the Word file **Letterhead** from the data files.

3. Compose a letter of transmittal dated October 1, 20--, to *Attention Mr. Wallace T. Brooks, Chairperson*. Check the Contacts list in Outlook for the address.

4. Use the information shown below to compose the letter:

    ¶1 State that the budget report for July 1, 20--, to June 30, 20--, is attached. The staff and the accountant for the city of New Orleans assisted Ms. McKay in the development of this budget.

    ¶2 Explain that ten budget categories are included, totaling the $2 million budget available for The Sports Connection. Note that all specifications required by the grant are incorporated in the proposed budget.

    ¶3 Refer to the meeting of the Community Foundation on Monday, October 12, at 7 p.m. Ms. McKay will give an oral presentation with PowerPoint slides to the Board of Directors.

5. Go to the first page of the report body in Section 2. View the report footer. Break the link between the footers in Sections 1 and 2 of the report. Close the footer.

6. Preliminary report pages should be numbered in lowercase Roman numerals centered in the footer. Go to the letter in Section 1 and view the footer. Insert the code for a page number. The letter will be numbered *i* for now. After you add a title page for the report, the letter will be page *ii*.

7. Remember to save your updates to the report.

TIPS

SOFTWARE

To break the link between the footers in Section 1 and Section 2, go to the Section 2 footer. Click the *Link with Previous* button on the Header and Footer toolbar.

3-4   **Design Title Page**

S O F T W A R E

Point to center of line and click once to enable the Click and Type feature. Double-click and key text.

- Design title page of report

The first impression the Community Foundation Board of Directors will have of this report is the title page. Therefore, do your best to design an attractive and professional title page.

1. Open the **Budget Report** Word file. Position the insertion point at the beginning of the document. Insert a manual page break.

2. At the top of the document, key the title page; use the Click and Type feature.

THE SPORTS CONNECTION BUDGET REPORT

Prepared for
Community Foundation Board of Directors

Prepared by
Ms. Karen McKay, Director

October 1, 20--

3. The title page is page i but should not display a number. If needed, modify the settings for Section 1 so the page number does not display. (*Hint:* Choose *Different first page* in the Page Setup dialog box.) Save the report.

Optional: Search the Internet for backgrounds, clip art, or borders to use on the title page or copy the logo art from the letter page.

3-5

Prepare List of Figures

- Prepare a list of figures

1. Open the **Budget Report** Word file.

2. Position the insertion point at the bottom of the letter of transmittal but above the section break. Insert a manual page break to create a new page in Section 1.

3. On the new page at about 2″ from the top, key *LIST OF FIGURES*. Tap *Enter* to create a new line. Apply Heading 1 style to the title text and center it.

4. To generate a list of figures.
   a. Choose *Insert, Reference, Index and Tables*.
   b. On the Table of Figures tab, check these options if they are not already selected:
      Show page numbers
      Right align page numbers
      Include label and number
   c. For the Tab leader option, the dotted line should be selected.
   d. Click *OK*.

5. Select the list of figures and change the line spacing to 2.

6. This should be page iii. Verify that the page number appears correctly at the bottom center of the page.

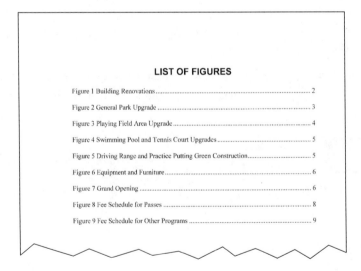

LIST OF FIGURES

Figure 1 Building Renovations...2
Figure 2 General Park Upgrade 3
Figure 3 Playing Field Area Upgrade..4
Figure 4 Swimming Pool and Tennis Court Upgrades..5
Figure 5 Driving Range and Practice Putting Green Construction...5
Figure 6 Equipment and Furniture..6
Figure 7 Grand Opening 6
Figure 8 Fee Schedule for Passes 8
Figure 9 Fee Schedule for Other Programs 9

3-6

Prepare Table of Contents

• Prepare a table of contents

1. Open the **Budget Report** Word file. Position the insertion point at the bottom of the letter of transmittal but above the section break. Insert a manual page break to create a new page in Section 1.

2. On the new page at about 2″ from the top, key *TABLE OF CONTENTS*. Tap *Enter* to create a new line. Apply Arial, bold, 16-point font to the title text and center it.

3. To generate a list of figures.
   a. Choose *Insert, Reference, Index and Tables.*
   b. On the Table of Contents tab, check these options if they are not already selected:
      Show page numbers
      Right align page numbers
   c. For the Tab leader option, the dotted line should be selected. For the Show levels option, enter *2*.
   d. Click *OK.*

4. Insert a hard return before each side heading, *Appendix A*, and *Appendix B.*

5. Edit *List of Figures, Appendix A*, and *Appendix B* to use initial caps for important words (instead of all caps). Edit the text to have only one entry for each appendix:
   Appendix A, Budget 11
   Appendix B, Grand Opening Expenditures 13

6. This page should be page iv. Verify again that the page numbers and page breaks throughout the report are appropriate. Make adjustments if needed.

7. Save and print the file.

3-7

Create Electronic Presentation

- Prepare an electronic presentation with clip art and sound files
- Embed and link files within a presentation
- Add hyperlinks to a presentation
- Hide slides
- Use AutoShapes
- Animate slides and use transitions

Design Template

Choose a design template for the presentation or design your own template.

Slide 1: Budget Report

Layout: *Title Slide*

Optional: Add appropriate graphic. Refer to Job 3-9 to locate graphics on the Web.

Slide 2: Topics

Layout: *Title and Text*

Slide 3: Budget Overview

Layout: *Title, Text, and Content*

1. Insert appropriate clip art.

2. Insert hyperlink to budget.
    a. Select the words *Budget Overview* in the title.
    b. Click *Insert, Hyperlink*.
    c. Link to file by clicking *Existing File or Web Page*. Locate the Excel file **Budget**. Click *OK*.

3. Set Custom Animation from Slideshow menu.
    a. Animate bulleted list.
    b. Select chime as sound.
    c. Set Blinds Horizontal as transition.

Slide 4: Bar Chart

Layout: *Blank*

1. Link to the Bar Chart sheet in the Excel file **Budget**.
    a. Open the bar chart. Click to select the entire chart. Click *Copy*.
    b. Go to Slide 4. Click *Edit, Paste Special*. Then click *Paste link*.

Note

The procedure for embedding and linking objects is almost the same except for choosing to Paste or Paste link.

*By choosing Paste link in Slide 4, you have set up a direct link to the Excel file **Budget**. When the budget is updated, Slide 4 is automatically updated as well.*

The Sports Connection
Budget Report

Submitted by
Karen McKay, Director

Slide 1

Topics

- Budget
- Fee Schedule
- Sponsorships
- Recommendation

Slide 2

Budget Overview

- Staff and city accountant's input
- Ten budget categories
- Grant specifications addressed

Slide 3

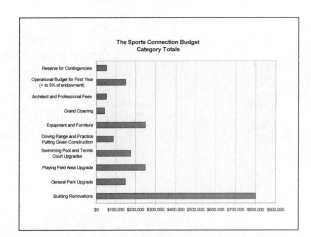

Slide 4

Slide 5: Budget Categories

Layout: *Title and 2-Column Text*

1. Key the ten budget categories.

2. Hide Slide 5: Go to Slide sorter view. Click the *Hide Slide* button to hide this slide.

   Ms. McKay does not wish to show a list of the ten budget categories. However, should a board member ask for a list, she can then show Slide 5.

Slide 6: Fee Schedule

Layout: *Title Only*

   This is all you can do on Slide 6 at this point. After all slides are prepared, you will add two hyperlinks to this slide that will take Ms. McKay directly to other slides in the presentation.

Slide 7: Sponsorships

Layout: *Title Only*

1. Create boxes using AutoShapes on the Drawing toolbar.
   a. Click *AutoShapes, Basic Shapes, Bevel* (third figure in fourth row).
   b. Right-click the box, click *Add Text*, and key the text.
   c. Change the font color to contrast with the box color, if necessary.
   d. Use the alignment tool to align both boxes.

2. Set Custom Animation to animate the two objects.

   Central University Athletic Department
   a. No sound.
   b. Entry: You choose the type of entry.
   c. Start: On Click

   First Bank
   a. No sound.
   b. Entry: You choose the type of entry.

3. Insert a sound.
   a. From the Insert menu, choose *Movies and Sounds*. Choose the *Sound from Clip Organizer* option.
   b. Enter *applause* in the *Search for* box and search. If this sound is not available, locate an applause sound on the Web. See Job 3-9 for instructions.
   c. Click the sound icon and move it to the bottom right corner of the screen. (Ms. McKay will click this icon after the discussion of two sponsors. The audience should join in with applause as well.)

3-7

Budget Categories

- Building renovations
- General park upgrade
- Playing field upgrade
- Swimming pool and tennis court upgrade
- Driving range/practice putting green construction
- Equipment/furniture
- Grand opening
- Architect and professional fees
- Operational budget for first year
- Reserve for contingencies

Slide 5

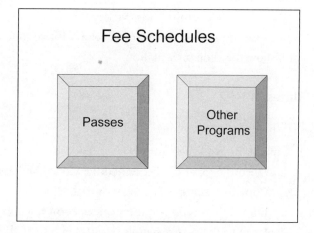

Slide 6

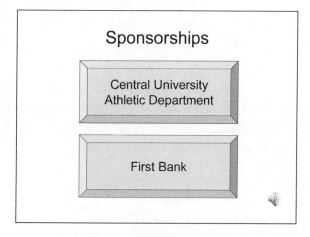

Slide 7

Slide 8: Recommendation

Layout: *Title, Content, and Text*

1. Insert appropriate clip art and key the text.

2. Set Custom Animation in this order:

   Bulleted List
   a. No sound.
   b. Entry: Zoom.
   c. After entry of bulleted item, have it dim to another color.

   Clip Art
   a. Start animation automatically 00:00 seconds after slide comes in.
   b. Entry animation and sound: Zoom.

Slide 9: Blank

Layout: *Blank*

The blank slide reminds Ms. McKay that this is the end of the presentation. *Optional*: Insert music here that would set a positive tone for the discussion period that will follow the slide presentation.

Slides: 10–12

Layout: *Title Only*

1. Embed the worksheet rows.
   a. Open the Excel file **Fee Schedule**. Go to the Passes sheet tab.
   b. Copy the appropriate range for each slide.
   c. Embed the portion of the worksheet on the appropriate slide.
   d. Point to the corner handle. Hold down the Ctrl key and size the object appropriately. (Be sure the object is large enough for the audience to view.)
   e. Double-click to edit object. Change the color of Row 1 to a color used in the template. Be sure to change the text or background color to contrast if necessary.

2. Create a Return Action Button on Slide 12.
   a. Click *Slide Show, Action Buttons*.
   b. Click the *Return* button. Drag and draw a small button at the bottom right of the slide.
   c. Choose *Hyperlink to* and then *Slide*. Choose *Slide 6 Fee Schedules*.

3-7

Recommendation

- Approval of budget
  - Improved facilities
  - New facilities
  - New sports events
  - Programming for disadvantaged
  - "Fitness for life" attitude

Slide 8

Slide 9

Types of Passes

Weekly Passes	Fee
Full access (no charge)	$0.00
Full access	$25.00
Fitness Center only	$15.00
Pool only	$12.00
Locker facilities	$8.00

Slide 10

Types of Passes

Monthly Passes	Fee
Full access (no charge)	$0.00
Full access	$60.00
Fitness Center only	$40.00
Pool only	$30.00
Locker facilities	$20.00

Slide 11

Types of Passes

Daily Passes	Fee
Pool	$5.00
Fitness Center	$10.00
Locker facilities	$2.00

Slide 12

Slide 13

Layout: *Title Only*

1. Embed the worksheet.
   a. In the Excel file **Fee Schedule,** go to the Other Programs sheet.
   b. Embed the appropriate portion of the worksheet.

2. Size and format the object appropriately.

Slide 14

Layout: *Title and 2-Column Text*

1. Key the bulleted lists.

2. Create *Return Action Button* to return to Slide 6 Fee Schedule.

Finish Slide 6

1. Insert hyperlinks.

   Passes
   a. Click *Slide Show, Action Buttons.*
   b. Click the *blank (Custom)* button. Drag and draw a button on the left side of
      the slide.
   c. Choose *Hyperlink to* and then *Slide.* Choose *Slide 10 Type of Passes.*

   Other Programs
   a. Repeat the steps above. Draw a button on the right side of the slide.
   b. Hyperlink to Slide 13 Other Programs. (*Hint:* Copy the first box and edit the
      hyperlink.)

2. Add text to the buttons.

Slide Transition

1. In Slide Sorter view, click *Ctrl+A* to select all slides.

2. Click the *Slide Transition* button. In the Slide Transition task pane, choose a slide
   transition that works well for this audience.

3. Save the file as **Budget Show**. You will print the slides in the next job.

Optional:

1. Create a footer to include the date of the presentation at the left margin and the
   slide number at the right margin of each slide.

2. Add appropriate clip art or a logo to appear on some slides.

3-7

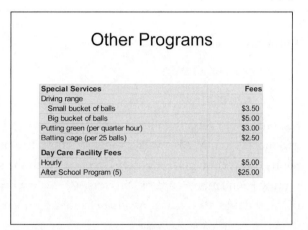

Slide 13

Slide 14

3-8

Prepare Fax Cover Sheet; Print Slides; Update Contacts List

- Use fax wizard to prepare a cover sheet

- Print handouts of slides

- Update Contacts list

Ms. McKay met Susan Walker, a multimedia consultant, at one of her speaking engagements recently. Ms. Walker was very supportive of the new programs at The Sports Connection and volunteered to assist with the slide presentation to the Community Foundation Board of Directors. Ms. McKay has asked you to fax a printout of the slides to Ms. Walker. Assume October 1 is today's date.

1. Use the fax wizard or a fax template to prepare the heading portion of the fax cover sheet to Ms. Susan Walker. When the wizard is finished, edit the heading to include all necessary information. Expand the placeholder so *The Sports Connection* fits on one line.

2. Compose the comments section of the cover sheet. Include the following points:
   a. State that printed slides for the speech to the Community Foundation Board of Directors are attached. Also, indicate that you are sending the PowerPoint file as an attachment to an e-mail message.
   b. Thank Ms. Walker for reviewing the slide presentation.
   c. End with a phone or fax number for her to return comments.
   d. Save the file using an appropriate name.

3. Print the **Budget Show** PowerPoint slides prepared in Job 3-7 as an audience handout—three slides to a page with lines printed at the right of each slide.

4. Add Ms. Walker's information to the General Contacts folder in Outlook.

   Ms. Susan Walker, Multimedia Consultant
   Walker Multimedia Company
   P.O. Box 9699
   New Orleans, LA 70115-9699
   Business Phone: (504) 555-0177
   Business Fax: (504) 555-0130
   E-mail: Swalker@ctec.net

5. If e-mail is available, send an e-mail message to your instructor and attach the PowerPoint file.

Optional Internet Activities: Clip Art, Photos, Sounds, and Motion Clips

3-9

• Visit an Internet site to find media clips

• Download clip art, photos, sound files, and motion clips from the Internet

• Insert clips into an electronic presentation

When working on presentations, newsletters, or other documents, you may have limited time to spend searching the Web for appropriate graphics or sound clips. Instead, you can visit the Microsoft Office Clip Art and Media site. This site can be accessed from the *Clip art on Office online* hyperlink shown in the Clip Art pane in PowerPoint, Word, and other Office programs. In this task, you will use this Web site to find clips to enhance the **Budget Show** presentation.

1. Open the **Budget Show** PowerPoint file.

2. Go to Slide 2. For this slide, find a photo of a group of people that could be working to determine a budget. Click the *Insert Clip Art* button on the Drawing toolbar. Click *Clip art on Office online* in the Clip Art task pane. (You must be connected to the Internet to use this hyperlink.)

3. Select *Photo* for the type of media you want to find. Enter one or two key words that describe the media in the search box and click *Go*. For example, you could key *business meeting* as the search term.

4. Browse the clips available. Click the check box under a clip to select it for downloading. After selecting clips, click *Download Now* (red arrow) to download the selected clips.

5. A screen will appear telling you the number of items selected for download and the size. Click *Download Now* to proceed. The clips will be saved to the Downloaded Clips folder in the Microsoft Clip Organizer.

6. From the Downloaded Clips folder in the Microsoft Clip Organizer, select a clip you downloaded. Click the down arrow and select *Insert* to place the clip on the slide.

(Cont. on next page)

7. Download and insert clips for these other slides:

   Slide 7: Search for an applause sound clip. Choose to have the sound play automatically and drag the sound clip off the slide.

   Slide 8: Choose another graphic that is appropriate for this slide.

   Slides 12 and 13: Locate motion clips to help the audience visualize these great activities (e.g. swimming, golf, baseball).

   Other: Locate one or more sports-related graphics to be used as design elements on all the slides after the title slide. Insert the graphic(s) in an appropriate location on the slide master. Add other enhancements of your choice to all or some slides.

8. Save the presentation as **Budget Show Revised**.

CRITICAL THINKING

Budgets

A **BUDGET** is a document that lists the expenditures a company or organization plans to make during a given period of time, often one year. A budget is based on the money that is expected to be available. The purpose of most budgets is to allocate spending in a rational manner to help accomplish the goals of the organization. Amounts for expenditures listed in the budget should be based on prior spending or research regarding costs for various items, activities, or projects. However, even with a well-planned budget, a surplus or a deficit (shortage) of funds can occur unless the spending is monitored carefully.

1. Ms. McKay will present the proposed budget for The Sports Connection to the Community Foundation Board of Directors for approval. You have become familiar with the budget as you prepared the worksheets, report, and presentation slides. What questions do you think the board members might ask Ms. McKay regarding the budget? How should Ms. McKay respond if she does not know the answer to a question?
2. Identify one or two budget items that you think could exceed the planned expenditures for those items. Give reasons why the amount of money needed for this item might be more than the amount budgeted. Tell what alternate plans could be made to keep the spending within the budgeted amounts.

Example:
Budget Item: Playing field upgrade
Reason: When working on the playing field upgrade, the contractor discovers a drainage problem that was not previously known.
Alternate Plans:
   o Relocate the playing field to another area that does not have a drainage problem.
   o Reallocate funds from another project to provide the additional money required.
   o Complete as much work on the field as the budgeted funds allow and delay completion of the project until next year.

© GETTY IMAGES/PHOTODISC

scenario

Still a key to the success of your office is your commitment to detail and to managing routine tasks. In this project, you see the need to compile (1) a listing of current employees with necessary data, (2) an agenda for a presentation, and (3) a directory of Advisory Council members for accessing from the intranet.

Today some of your time will be spent updating The Sports Connection databases. Your knowledge of database software is certainly an asset in your position. Do remember to update the calendar and the tasks list. Thanks for your great work.

profile

Managing Routine Tasks

project

4

4-1

Create and Sort Table

- Key table from unarranged copy

- Sort table

- Format using AutoFormat

1. Organize the handwritten data on the following page as a table. Enter the names so they may be sorted easily by surname. Include the title as part of the table.

2. Add your information as a salaried assistant director.

3. Sort by last name of employee.

4. Use the AutoFormat feature to format the table attractively. Choose a format that will be attractive and easy to read.

5. Save the table as **Employees**.

4-1

Current Employees

Heath Bradley

289-01-0298

Maintenance

40 hours per week

Alam Khoo

932-02-3816

Event Coordinator

40 hours per week

Chad Kihlken

732-32-0038

Recreational Supervisor

25 hours per week

Tonya Collum

532-76-2039

Recreational Supervisor

15 hours per week

Karen McKay

189-32-9323

Director

Salary

Gregory Rickert

932-17-9337

Night Security

40 hours per week

Molly Neely

532-77-2443

Receptionist

40 hours per week

Renea Hinnant

654-29-9734

Recreational Supervisor

20 hours per week

Ryan Sykes

654-78-0932

Recreational Supervisor

20 hours per week

4-2

Prepare Agenda

- Key agenda

- Use copy and paste feature

- Print and arrange for copying

Prepare an agenda for the presentation to the Community Foundation Board of Directors on October 22. Use the headings in the report (Job 3-1) as the agenda items. Refer to the agenda at the right as a sample, but use your own creativity in creating an attractive design. Ms. McKay's goal is to provide the members of the Community Foundation Board of Directors a listing of the topics to be covered and space for writing questions or comments.

(*Reminder:* Save keying time and proofreading time by using Copy and Paste to copy the agenda items from the **Budget Report** file (Job 3-1).)

Place the *Additional Information* section on a second page. Print the second page of the agenda on the back of the first page for duplex copying for the meeting.

Print the two fee schedule worksheets from the Excel **Fee Schedule** file (Job 2-4) and attach them to the agenda.

SOFTWARE TIPS

Display Clipboard
Edit menu, Office
Clipboard

4~2

The Sports Connection

Presentation to the
Community Foundation Board of Directory

August 15, 20--

Agenda	Questions/Comments
Accomplishments New director announced Assistant director position being advertised Initial meetings with mayor and city council, architects, and university officials **Short-Term Goals** Finalize budget Employ assistant director and sports directors Plan grand opening	

Additional Information

4-3

Edit, Sort, and Query Database; Create Reports

Sponsors

- Add and delete records

- Modify the structure of a database

- Create and print reports for labels

- Sort data in database reports and tables

- Run a query and print the results table

One of your responsibilities as assistant director of The Sports Connection is to manage the databases of The Sports Connection. A number of changes to the **Sponsors** database file are needed.

1. Open the **Sponsors** Access file. In the *Sponsors* table, delete records for the following companies that went out of business: Tours, Inc. and Saints Clothing.

2. Delete the following fields that are no longer needed: *Type of Business* and *Employees*.

3. Add new records for sponsors who have responded with donations as shown on the following page. (*Hint:* Use an AutoForm to make entering data easier. Do not save the AutoForm.)

4. Make the changes in records as shown on the following page.

5. Use the Label Wizard to create reports for mailing labels and file folder labels for all records in the *Sponsors* table.
   - Use *English* for Unit of Measure and Avery 5162, 1 1/3″ x 4″. Use an Arial, 11-point font. Include the fields shown in the illustration below. Sort the mailing labels in postal code order. Name the report *Mailing Labels Sponsors*.

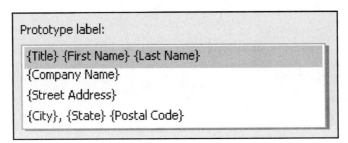

Prototype label:

{Title} {First Name} {Last Name}
{Company Name}
{Street Address}
{City}, {State} {Postal Code}

   - For the file folder labels, use *English* for Unit of Measure and Avery Index Maker 3 Tab. Include only the Company Name field. Sort the file labels in alphabetical order. Name the report *File Labels Sponsors*.
   - Print the mailing labels and the file labels.

Hide Columns
Format menu, Hide
Columns

6. Sort the *Sponsors* table by the Contribution field in descending order and print it in landscape orientation. To ensure that the table will fit on one page, hide the following columns before printing: Title, Position, City, State, Date Contacted, Response. Unhide the columns after printing.

7. Run the *$5,000+ Sponsors* query; then print the results table.

New records:

1. Mr. Lee Marks, Manager of the Trophy Shop, a retail business with 10 employees, located at 3485 Harmony St., New Orleans, 70115-3857, contacted on 11/14, donated $5,000. Contact numbers: 504-555-0148, FAX 504-555-0144.

2. Ms. Mary Glenn, a partner in Murphy & Glenn, PA, a law firm located at 75 Royal St., New Orleans, 70130-4294, contacted on 11/20, donated $1,000. Contact numbers: 504-555-0147, FAX 504-555-0143.

3. Ms. Jane Bass, Editor of City Guide, a magazine publisher located at 285 Beck St., New Orleans, 70110-4865, contacted on 11/24, donated $6,500. Contact numbers: 504-555-0146, FAX 504-555-0142.

4. Mr. Charles Horn, owner of C. H. Tees, a retail shop located at 1101 Bienville St., New Orleans, 70102-3984, contacted on 11/26, donated $250. Contact numbers: 504-555-0145, FAX 504-555-0141.

Changes in records:

1. Jon Bauer of LA Savings Bank was promoted to Senior V.P.

2. Price's Shoes moved to its new location at 750 St. Charles; all other information remains the same.

3. Grants Oil, Inc. provided another gift of $1,000. Update the record to show the total amount of both gifts.

4. The Sports Locker Co. bought out Good Sports Inc. Enter the combined gift amounts in The Sports Locker Co. record. Ms. Ortiz remains the contact. Delete the Good Sports Inc. record.

Update Calendar

- Schedule appointments and print daily calendar
- Enter tasks with priorities

You consider scheduling appointments and monitoring progress on projects to be very important and carry out these responsibilities with accuracy, completeness, and tact. Ms. McKay has thanked you for the positive public relations you are building through this commitment to your clients and guests.

ENTER APPOINTMENTS

Make the following entries in Ms. McKay's calendar, all with a Business label:

October 4   *Meeting with Wallace Brooks, CF Director, his office, 11 a.m. Allow one hour for this appointment.*

Lunch meeting with L. N. Skipwith, Mayor, and Wallace Brooks, The Island Restaurant, 12:30 reservation. Allow two hours for this lunch meeting. Add note: Reservation for three made on 9/28 in McKay's name.

October 7   *Meeting with Barbara Thrasher, Senior Women's Administrator, Central University Athletic Department, about the new girls' soccer program, Ms. McKay's office, 9 a.m. Allow one hour.*

October 8   *Meeting with Stan Williams, Ms. McKay's office, 1 p.m. Allow 30 minutes for this appointment.*

Move appointment with Barbara Thrasher on 10/7 at 9 a.m. to today (10/8) at 2 p.m.

Cancel the appointment with Stan Williams on 10/8.

ENTER TASKS

1. Mark the following tasks completed.
   Formal Report and Presentation to Community Foundation Board of Directors, due 9/20
   Celebrate Fitness Week, due 4/2
   New Fitness Staff Orientation, due 2/17

2. For the *Plan Grand Opening* task, change the percent complete to *50%*. In the text area, add *Special Entertainment* under *Program*.

3. Add a new task: *Article for The Sports Connection Web Site*. The start date is October 13 and the due date is October 29. Make this *Normal* priority with the status being *In Progress*. Percent complete is *25%*.

PRINT CALENDAR

Print the calendar in daily style (1 page/day) for October 4 and in tri-fold style for each day October 4-8. Include a footer to show Ms. McKay's name, the page number, and the date printed.

4-5

Design Directory for Intranet

- Create directory using mail merge

- Format directory as an attractive Web page

- Post to intranet (optional)

You will recall that the grant specified that an Advisory Council be established to oversee the financial and operational activities. In the Software Training Manual, you set up a Contacts folder for listing potential members of the Advisory Council from your community. Today a five-member Advisory Council has been approved. You have been asked to prepare an attractive directory that will be posted on The Sports Connection intranet.

Members of the Advisory Council are:

1. Physician with interest in sports medicine you selected

2. Accountant you selected

3. Sports professional you selected

4. Dr. Barbara Thrasher, Senior Women's Administrator, Central University Athletics Department (see the General Contacts folder for information)

5. Corporate executive you selected

Use the Mail Merge feature and your Contacts list to create an attractive telephone directory for posting on The Sports Connection intranet. Include the Last, First, and Phone fields.

Task 1: Move Contact to Advisory Council Folder

1. Start Outlook. Display the list of folders in the Navigation pane.

2. Open the General Contacts folder. Select the entry for Barbara Thrasher and drag it to the Advisory Council folder. Close Outlook.

Task 2: Merge with Outlook Advisory Council Contacts List

1. Open a new blank document in Word. Click *Tools, Letters and Mailings, Mail Merge*. Select *Directory* as the main document type. Use the current document.

2. Follow the prompts in the Mail Merge pane to choose recipients from an Outlook Contacts folder. Select the Advisory Council folder. Select all the records and sort by the *Last* field.

3. Continue to follow the prompts. Insert the *Last* merge field, type a comma, space, and insert the *First* merge field.

4. Use the Tabs dialog box (*Format, Tabs*) to set a right tab at position *6* with a dot leader (click *2* in the Leader section). Press *Tab* to move the insertion point to the new tab stop.

5. Insert the *Phone* merge field at the tab position, and tap *Enter* so that each telephone number appears on a separate line.

6. Merge to a new document. Save the merged document as **Ad Council Phone List.**

Task 2: Format Web Document

1. Edit the merged document to include *ADVISORY COUNCIL PHONE DIRECTORY* as the main heading.

2. To format the document attractively, choose an attractive theme or add formats of your choice to enhance this document's appearance on the intranet. Suggestions include
   - Lines
   - Fonts that are interesting and easy to read
   - Appropriate font size for easy reading
   - Attractive text color and background color
   - Character effects
   - Text effects, such as animation

3. Save the document as a single file Web page (click *File, Save as Web Page*). Change the page title to *Advisory Council Phone Directory*. Name the file **Ad Council Web Directory.**

4. View the Web page for appearance. Edit as needed and resave.

5. If you have a Web site, post the document to the Web site. (Private information should not be posted unless permission has been granted.)

4-6   Modify a Table

- Format a table with borders and shading

- Add and delete table rows

1. Open the **Employees** table you created in Job 4-1. Save the table as **Employees Updated (current date).** (Insert the current month, day, and year in the file-name, such as *10-11-06*.)

2. Remove the AutoFormat you previously applied. Format the table attractively using the Borders and Shading option on the Format menu.

3. Insert a new row above *Ryan Sykes*. Move Tonya Collum's information to the new row, but use the new name *Tonya Summers*. (*Hint:* Use Cut and Paste.) Delete the row that previously contained Tonya Collum's information.

CRITICAL THINKING

Database Queries

ONE OF your responsibilities as assistant director is to manage the databases for The Sports Connection. Your goal is to be able to provide information quickly and update the data efficiently. You have used a select query to find information—records of sponsors who donated $5,000 or more. You want to investigate other ways queries can be used to help you manage data. You realize that you can learn from the Access Help documentation and improve your software skills.

1. Suppose you have a database table that lists all the classes scheduled at The Sports Connection for the next three months. The deadline for registering for the classes has passed. You want to delete all records for classes that have no participants registered. What type of query could you use to accomplish this task?
2. Suppose you have a database table that contains the fee charged for each class offered by The Sports Connection. Ms. McKay has informed you that all fees will be increased by 10 percent. What type of query could you use to change the fee amounts in the table?
3. Suppose you have a database table that contains the names, addresses, and other information for students registered for a class at The Sports Connection. You want to add that information to a table that contains records for everyone who receives The Sports Connection newsletter. What type of query could you use to accomplish this task?

4-7

Optional Internet Activities: Sports Information

- Locate resources on the Internet
- Set bookmarks

Task 1: Sports Resources

Ms. McKay has asked you to start locating Internet sites for sports information that would be good resources for newsletters, handouts, and ideas for activities.

1. Access the Internet and open a search engine site. Use the search engine to find the Web site addresses for ESPN.com and CBS Sportsline.

2. Visit each of the sites and set a bookmark for each site. Visit several of the links at each site to become familiar with the information that is available.

Task 2: Sports Injuries

Several members of the Advisory Council asked if you had information on the sports whose participants are likely to have the most injuries. You want to be prepared to answer their questions.

1. Access the Internet and open a search engine site. Use the search engine to find the Web site address for the National Collegiate Athletics Association.

2. Access the site and search to find information about sports injuries. Print information showing data about injuries in various sports.

© GETTY IMAGES/PHOTODISC

scenario

profile

As assistant director, you have major responsibility for the grand opening of The Sports Connection. You will prepare numerous documents, including memos, Excel worksheets, PowerPoint presentations, form letters, newsletters, and invitations. To manage these documents, you decide to set up an electronic folder for keeping track of all these documents.

In Project 5 you prepare the budget for the grand opening, the initial memo to the Grand Opening Committee, and an electronic presentation to be used to orient various groups to the grand opening activities. Updates to the calendar are always your responsibility.

project

Planning the Grand Opening

5

5-1

Create Worksheet

- Create a worksheet from unarranged copy

- Enter formulas in a worksheet

- Enter comments in a worksheet

- Format a worksheet attractively

The budget prepared in Project 2 shows expenses budgeted for the grand opening. Ms. McKay has requested a worksheet that shows a more detailed breakdown of these expenses. Refer to the budget to be sure you are not exceeding the overall budget amount for this category. If cuts are necessary, decrease the amount designated for tee shirts. Format the worksheet attractively. Use Format Painter to speed up your work.

SOFTWARE

To insert the current date, use the formula =TODAY().

1. Open the Excel file **Budget**. Insert a new blank worksheet and name it *Grand Opening Expenses*. Enter the data shown on the following page. In Cell A2, insert the date as the sheet subtitle. Leave Row 3 blank.

2. Key formulas in Column C for calculating the following:
   - Subtotals for each budget category
   - The Grand Opening budget total

3. Compare the total for the Grand Opening budget on this sheet with the Grand Opening subtotal on the Budget sheet. If necessary, adjust the Grand Opening budget to be in line with the subtotal on the Budget sheet.

4. Format this sheet to match the Budget sheet. Set the top margin to 2″ and center horizontally on the page.

5. Key these comments in the designated cells:

Cell Contents	*Comment*
Food	*Barbecue sandwiches, chips, potato salad, cole slaw (1/2 donated by local restaurant)*
Soft drinks and cups	*1/2 donated by local bottling company*

6. Access the *Sheet* tab in the Page Setup dialog box. Select the option to have comments print at the end of the sheet.

5-1

Grand Opening Expenses

Printing

    Invitations (3500)
    Newsletter (4000)
    Program (2000)

Mailings

    Paper (1000)
    Postage (1500)

Advertisement

    Newspaper ads (150)
    Tee Shirts with logos (2200)

Decorations

    Banners (375)
    Balloons (75)
    Tablecloths (200)

Picnic

    Food (10000)
    Soft drinks and cups (2000)

Speaker

    Speaker's fee (5000)
    Travel (800)
    Hotel and meals (200)

Entertainment   (7000)

5-2

Update Calendar and Contacts List; Display Map

- Schedule appointment as a recurring meeting

- Update Contacts folder

Task 1: Update Calendar

Make the following entry in Ms. McKay's calendar. Print the calendar for October 19 in daily style.

> *October 19 Business meeting with Grand Opening Committee, Conference Room, 9 a.m. Allow 1 1/2 hours. Make this a weekly recurring meeting.*

Task 2: Update Contacts List

Add the following three people from the Grand Opening Committee to the General Contacts folder. Print the General Contacts folder entries in card style.

Mr. L. N. Skipwith, Mayor
New Orleans City Hall
4963 Main Street
New Orleans, LA 70115-0024
Business Phone: (504) 555-0195
Business Fax: (504) 555-0196
E-mail: Lskipwith@city.hall

Ms. Marilyn Cade
Chamber of Commerce
New Orleans City Hall, Room 343
4963 Main Street
New Orleans, LA 70115-0024
Business Phone: (504) 555-0167
Business Fax: (504) 555-0168
E-mail: Mcade@city.hall

Mr. Wayne Cobill
Central University, University Relations Office
23 Easton Boulevard
New Orleans, LA 70115-0023
Business Phone: (504) 555-0121
Business Fax: (504) 555-0120
E-mail: Wcobill@central.edu

Task 3: Display Map (optional)

Ms. McKay needs directions to the office of the accountant listed in the Advisory Council contacts list. Use Outlook to display and print a map to this address. Refer to Software Training Manual, p. 141.

5-3

Set Up Electronic Folder for Grand Opening

- Create folder

- Add file to folder

A common practice for organizing various documents all related to a project is to keep them in an electronic folder named appropriately for the project or activity. Microsoft Windows software provides Windows Explorer to assist in effective electronic file management.

Because you will be creating a number of documents related to the grand opening, create a folder named *Grand Opening Project*. Follow the steps below to create the folder and to move the Excel file **Budget** to this folder.

CREATE FOLDER

1. Open Windows Explorer (*Start, My Computer*).

2. Double-click the drive where the folder is to be created.

3. Click *File, New,* and then *Folder*.

4. Key a name for the folder: *Grand Opening Project*. Tap *Enter*.

MOVE FILE TO THE FOLDER

1. In Windows Explorer, navigate to the folder where your Excel file **Budget** is stored. Click the file once to select it.

2. Under File and Folder Tasks, click *Move this file*. In the Move Items dialog box, select the *Grand Opening Project* folder. Click *Move*.

In the future, when you need to edit documents related to the grand opening, open the Grand Opening Project folder. In fact, while in Windows Explorer, you can double-click to open the desired file. The application (PowerPoint, Excel, Access, etc.) will open, and then the desired file will open.

5-4

Format Table

- Use AutoFormat

- Add enhancements

Create a Grand Opening Events table, using the information shown on the following page. Because you may use this table as a printed flyer, format it attractively.

1. Set a left tab in Column 1 at .15″ and use it to indent items as marked.

2. Apply the *Table Simple 3* AutoFormat to the table. Apply bold and center to the column headings. Center the table horizontally on the page.

3. Save the document as **Grand Opening Events** in the Grand Opening Projects folder.

C R I T I C A L THINKING

Committee Meetings

IN THIS project, you created a recurring appointment for Ms. McKay to meet weekly with the members of the Grand Opening Committee. As the assistant director, you will also attend these meetings. When leading the meetings, Ms. McKay will need to keep the discussion focused and seek input from all of the committee members.

1. Although most meetings are held for a specific purpose, the attention and comments of the people participating may wander to other topics. Personal comments or comments about community events or work-related matters can take valuable time planned to be devoted to the meeting topic. What strategies can Ms. McKay use to keep the discussion focused on the planned meeting topics while keeping the tone of the meeting friendly?
2. The Grand Opening Committee has members from various organizations and positions of authority. Some committee members may hesitate to express their ideas because they are awed or a bit intimated by other members. What strategies can Ms. McKay use to make all members realize that their input is important?
3. Some committee members may dominate the discussion, questions, or suggestions on topics brought up at a meeting. What strategies can Ms. McKay use to discourage a person who is dominating the discussion while keeping this person's goodwill?

5-4

Keep the title within the table.

Grand Opening Events — *12 pt*

Set a left tab to indent

Event	Location	Time
Television Interview Wallace Brooks Mayor Skipwith Karen McKay Recreational supervisor Members (selected)	Main lobby—Sports Connection	5:00 a.m. (To be aired at 6 a.m., 6 p.m., and 10 p.m.)
Aerobics Special Function Speaker leads class	Aerobics Classroom	8:00 - 9:00 a.m.
Tour of The Sports Connection	Begins at main lobby	9:00 - 10:45 a.m.
Dignitaries' Reception	Conference Room	9:30 - 10:30 a.m.
Grand Opening Ceremony Ribbon Cutting Speaker	Big Tent on facility grounds	11:00 - 11:45 a.m.
Picnic Barbecue Entertainment	Facility grounds	12:00 - 2:00 p.m.
Soccer Tournament	Soccer fields	2:30 - 6:00 p.m.

Adjust Column width so events are on one line.

- Add a hard return at the end of each row to separate events.

- Center table vertically.

Key Memo and Assemble Documents

- Add memo to folder

- Use memo template

- Create table

- Embed worksheet

1. Using the Professional Memo template, prepare the memo shown on page 73 that (1) calls a meeting of the committee, (2) outlines the committee's goals, and (3) includes a table and worksheet for the members to review prior to the first meeting. Address the memo to the Grand Opening Committee. The memo is from Karen McKay and should be dated October 8.

2. Insert the table created earlier that lists the grand opening events where indicated. Check the formatting when it displays in the memo and make whatever adjustments are necessary.

3. Below your reference initials, list in alphabetical order the names of the committee members from the table below (including Ms. McKay) as a distribution list. Change the spacing after each item to 2 points.

4. Delete the footer on each page. Add a second-page memo heading in the header on page 2 only:
Grand Opening Committee
Page 2
October 8, 200-

5. Save the memo as **Grand Opening Memo** 10-8 in the Grand Opening Project folder.

(Cont. on next page)

6. Print the Excel workbook **Budget** (all sheets). Assemble the documents, placing the Grand Opening Budget worksheet behind the printed memo as the enclosure. Staple The Sports Connection Budget and the two charts together; hold them until requested by your instructor.

5-5

Grand Opening Committee	
Name	**Organization Representing**
Karen McKay	Chairperson and Director
Wallace Brooks	Chairperson, Community Foundation
L. N. Skipwith	Mayor
Your Name	Assistant Director
Marilyn Cade	Chamber of Commerce
Wayne Cobill	Central University, University Relations
Alam Khoo	Recreational Supervisor
Renea Hinnant	Recreational Supervisor
Chad Kihlken	Recreational Supervisor

Thank you for agreeing to serve on the Grand Opening Committee of The Sports Connection. Our mission is to plan a comprehensive grand opening that will generate awareness of The Sports Connection and its programs. We also want to create a desire in individuals to purchase memberships in our facility and for youth to enroll in our varied sports teams. The Grand Opening should help the community to know about our mission to promote good sportsmanship, fitness, good health, and recreational activities. But more importantly, the Grand Opening will spark our citizens and their children and grandchildren to take advantage of these many outstanding programs.

A list of the members of the Grand Opening Committee is shown at the bottom of this page. We are very fortunate to have Mr. Wallace Brooks serve on this committee. Mr. Brooks worked with the development of the grant that funded the improvements and additions to The Sports Connection. He presently serves as chair of The Community Foundation that oversees this grant. Also, we appreciate the support of the Chamber of Commerce and the university relations office of Central University. Thank you, Marilyn and Wayne, for the expertise and experience you bring to this committee. Mayor Skipwith or one of his officials will also represent the mayor's office. Lastly, my assistant director and three of the recreational supervisors will bring their knowledge of The Sports Connection and the recreational programs to our committee.

The first official meeting of the Grand Opening Committee is scheduled for Tuesday, October 19, at 9 a.m. in the Conference Room of The Sports Connection. Based on our phone survey, we have determined Tuesdays at 9 to be a suitable time for this committee to meet each week. Please mark your calendars to meet each Tuesday from 9:00 — 10:30 until the Grand Opening. For your convenience, our staff will provide coffee and a light brunch at each meeting. A telephone is also located in the Conference Room should your office need to reach you; the number is 555-0141.

During the last few weeks, my assistant and I have compiled grand opening plans of other sports facilities. During this process we have garnered advice from these planners and will benefit from their experience. The following table outlines a list of suggested events from which our committee can begin. Please review this table prior to our first meeting. Bring to the meeting any additions and/or modifications to

(Insert File events and the time table.

5-4 Table.doc
here.)   A draft of the Grand Opening budget is enclosed. Please review the items to be sure all expenses are listed and that the budgeted amounts are in line with today's costs. Please bring your comments to the meeting so that adjustments to the budget can be made and the budget approved. I appreciate your commitment to this committee and look forward to working with each of you.

5-6

Design Electronic Presentation

- Add presentation to folder

- Choose design template

- Create predesigned slides

- Design new slides

- Animate text and objects

- Select slide transitions

At its first meeting, the Grand Opening Committee recommended that a Power-Point presentation be developed that explains the plans for the grand opening of The Sports Connection. Possible audiences include the Community Foundation Board of Directors, the Chamber of Commerce, hospital administration, staff of The Sports Connection, city officials, and local sports associations.

Choose an appropriate PowerPoint design template. You may also design your own template or modify an existing template. Create a footer that includes the slide number at the right of each slide. When you have created all of the slides as directed on the following two pages, complete the presentation as follows:

- Add sound to enhance the presentation.

- Choose transitions effectively to bring in bulleted lists.

- Choose slide transitions effectively to move from one slide to the next.

Save the presentation as **Grand Opening Plans** in the Grand Opening Project folder.

Slide 1

Layout: *Title Slide*

Compose a title for this presentation. Review the purpose of this presentation and be reminded of your audiences. Include the date of the event, April 15, 20--.

Optional: Search the Internet for appropriate clip art or images to enhance the title page.

Slide 2: Our Facility

Layout: *Title, Text, and Content*

Key the following bulleted list on the left side of the slide:

Building renovations
General park upgrade
Playing fields upgrade
Swimming pool and tennis courts upgrades
Driving range/putting green construction
Equipment and furniture

Insert an image of a sports facility on the right side of the slide. You may (1) locate an appropriate image via the Internet, (2) scan an image from a magazine or newspaper, or (3) use a digital camera to take a photograph of a local sports facility.

Slide 3: Schedule of Events

Layout: *Content*

Create the following table. Change the text color to an appropriate color for viewers.

TV Interview	5 a.m.
Aerobics Feature	8 a.m.
Tours	9:00–10:45 a.m.
Dignitaries' Reception	9:30–10:30 a.m.
Opening Ceremony	11:00–11:45 a.m.
Picnic	12 noon
Soccer Tournament	2:30 p.m.

Slide 4: Grand Opening Expenses

Layout: *Blank*

Embed the pie chart created in Project 2 in the **Budget** Excel file on this blank slide. Size the chart to cover most of the slide. Add a border or background, if desired, for an attractive slide.

(Cont. on next page)

Slide 5: Printing

Layout: *Title and Text*

    Key the three printing expenses as a bulleted list. Insert an object or graphic that reminds viewers of the category. Display the budgeted amount in a creative way. Set the animation so the budgeted amount will display with a mouse click.

Slides 6–11

Repeat the directions for Slide 5 for each of the seven budget categories. (*Hint:* After creating the Printing slide, insert a duplicate slide and edit it for the new budget category.) On the Entertainment slide, list two or three types of entertainment that might be provided such as music, games, and clowns.

Slide 12: Web Sites

Layout: *Title and Text*

    Locate one or more appropriate Web sites that Ms. McKay might want to go to during a presentation discussing the grand opening events. In a bulleted list, key the Web site addresses. Make each address a hyperlink to that Web site. (*Hint:* Review the Web sites you found in Job 4-7.)

Slides 13–14

Create at least two additional slides for the electronic presentation. Review the information about the grand opening events from the previous jobs and identify content that Ms. McKay might want to present or have ready in answer to questions from the audience.

    Include ample white space on each slide; avoid a cluttered slide. Use pictures, video, or sound clips from the Clip Organizer or the Internet to enhance the slides where appropriate.

Optional Internet Activities: Design Master Title Slide and Background

- Locate appropriate graphics and sound files on the Internet

- Download information from the Web

- Create master title slide and background using graphics and sounds

You have been asked to present a short speech of your choice at one of your monthly meetings (e.g., civic club, literary club, garden club, public speaking club, professional association, etc.). You realize that the opening slide must be very interesting to capture the attention of the audience and set the tone of the presentation. Therefore, you will design a creative master title slide and background.

Task 1: Create Master Title Slide

Choose Presentation Topic

Choose one of the presentation topics listed below:

- Any sport

- Fitness and nutrition

- First aid

- Coaching youth sports teams

- Other topic approved by your instructor

Locate Relevant Graphics

Search the Internet for appropriate graphics for the title slide. Your design may include a logo that could display on every slide, a photo, clip art, border, or motion clip.

Design Title Slide

Use your creativity and knowledge of PowerPoint to design an original background for the title slide. Create this design on the master title slide (*View, Master, Slide Master*).

1. Insert the graphics you located on the Internet. Size and place the graphics attractively. Add a footer that includes *The Sports Connection* and the slide number.

2. Key a title that will engage your audience in your topic. Key the subtitle *Presented by (Your Name)*. You may also wish to record the title or an opening statement to play with the title slide.

3. Save the presentation file using an appropriate name.

SOFTWARE TIPS

To apply gradient, texture, pattern, or picture effects, choose *Format, Background, Fill Effects*.

(Cont. on next page)

Task 2: Add Music to Title Slide

You are very pleased with the title slide you prepared in Task 1. Now you need appropriate sound files to use either at the beginning of the presentation, during the presentation, and/or at the conclusion of the presentation.

Locate Sound Files for Presentation

Search on your local or network drive or on the Internet for an appropriate sound file for the title slide. For example, **Beethoven.wav** is a sound file that could be used as the slide transition for an opening slide.

Insert Sounds on Slides

1. Open the presentation started in Job 5-7, Task 1. (If you did not complete Job 5-7, Task 1, open a blank presentation.)

2. Select a sound to play with the slide transition as the title slide opens. This can be a sound, such as *Drum Roll* or *Chime,* that is available from the Sound drop-down list or a sound file you downloaded from the Internet or other source. To use a downloaded file, choose *Other Sound* from the Sound drop-down list in the Slide Transition pane. Navigate to the folder where the file is stored and select the file.

3. Insert sounds on other slides, using sound files available on your computer or ones you have downloaded. The sounds can be part of the slide transition or set to play on a mouse click.

Task 3: Play CD

Presentations often will include music in the background as a slide show is being displayed. Open one of the PowerPoint presentations you have completed in this simulation. Insert a music CD in your computer. Follow these steps to play the CD during the presentation:

1. Go to Slide 1.

2. Choose *Insert, Movies and Sounds, Play CD Audio Track.*

3. Choose the track(s) to be played. Select *Loop until stopped* if you want the selection to start over when it has finished playing.

4. Adjust the sound volume appropriately for the slide presentation.

5. Play the slide show.

6-1 Design invitation

6-2 Develop article from outline

6-3 Develop strategy for advertising flyer

6-4 Prepare newsletter

6-5 Optional Internet activities

© GETTY IMAGES/PHOTODISC

scenario

Ms. McKay asked you to take responsibility for designing the documents that will be used to publicize the grand opening of The Sports Connection. She asked that you get ideas from members of the Grand Opening Committee who have worked closely as a team to plan the grand opening. Then she would like you to use your excellent research skills, desktop publishing skills, and creativity to design attractive documents to publicize the grand opening.

At its last meeting, the Grand Opening Committee agreed that four documents were essential for the grand opening—an invitation to the event, a newspaper article focusing on the benefits of participating in sports, a flyer announcing the grand opening, and a newsletter.

profile

project

Designing Publicity Pieces

6

6-1   **Design Invitation**

• Apply creativity to design invitation

After meeting with the Grand Opening Committee, you are now ready to design the invitation to the Grand Opening Ceremony. The local utility companies have agreed to include the invitation as an insert in the bills that they mail out the month prior to the event provided that it is printed on a standard size sheet of regular weight paper (so that it can be folded automatically with other items included in the bill).

You will also place the invitation as an ad in the local newspaper to publicize the event. The committee looked at a number of invitations and liked the general appearance of the one shown below. Include the information shown at the right.

Dedication
The Community Concert Hall

You are cordially invited to attend

the dedication of

The Community Concert Hall

4200 Canal Street

Saturday, July 22, 20--

seven o'clock

Dedication Ceremony

Tour of New Facilities

Reception

RSVP 555-0182

6-1

Grand Opening
The Sports Connection

You are cordially invited to attend | the grand opening celebration of | The Sports Connection | 5600 St. Charles Avenue | Saturday, April 15, 20-- | ten o'clock | Dedication Ceremony | Tour of New Facilities | Picnic Lunch | RSVP 555-0139

6-2   Develop Article from Outline

- Research topic using the Internet and local resources

- Compose article from outline

Prepare an article about the benefits of participating in sports that will be published in the local newspaper. You asked the Grand Opening Committee to suggest ideas for the article. The committee helped you develop the title and the informal outline on the following page. Use the Internet and local resources to get additional information you need to compose the article.

Follow these guidelines for the article:

- The length of the article should be about two double-spaced pages.

- Use WordArt for the title.

- Include an appropriate clip art image near the title.

- Use an 11-point or 12-point font for the body and paragraph styles for all headings in the article.

- Create a footer to include the date and time, using the Date and Time feature.

6~2

Who, Me? Participate in Sports?

Introductory section
- Sports are for everyone, not just the super athlete
- Sports are for both male and female, young and old
- Key is to find the sports that appeal to you

Sports are fun
- Enjoy the company of current friends
- Meet new friends
- Do things you enjoy doing

Sports promote fitness
- Sports help you get in shape
- Sports help you stay in shape
- Sports involve exercise that relieves stress
- Sports help with weight control

Sports help develop critical job skills
- Sports help you develop leadership skills
- Sports help you develop teamwork skills

6-3

Develop Strategy for Advertising Flyer

- Determine strategy for number of flyers needed

- Compose appropriate flyer(s)

- Format flyer(s) using desktop publishing skills

Design an attractive flyer that can be posted in prominent places to announce the grand opening of The Sports Connection. The flyer will be posted in a number of locations, including local businesses, government offices, schools, church recreation halls, and other public places. The purpose of the flyer is more of a reminder of the event than an invitation. Most of the people who are likely to attend have already received an invitation. Use clip art and make sure the print can be read from a distance.

The flyer should appeal to a number of different audiences, including:

- Young people who will participate in The Sports Connection activities.

- Parents who may encourage their children to participate.

- Volunteers who might be willing to coach or work in other capacities.

- Businesses and other organizations that may be willing to sponsor activities.

- Individuals who may be willing to serve on the Advisory Council.

Task 1: Determine Best Strategy—Single Flyer or Multiple Versions

- Can one flyer appeal to all of the individuals listed above?

- Would separate flyers be more effective?

Task 2: Make and Justify Decision

- If you choose to use one version, prepare a brief justification explaining why you think the flyer will be effective for all the groups listed.

- If you choose to prepare multiple versions, explain to whom each version is designed to appeal and why you think it will be effective.

Task 3: Determine Content

How much and what types of information must be included? Key the information for the flyer(s) in unarranged format.

Task 4: Prepare the Flyer(s)

Format the flyer(s) in an attractive style. Use visual enhancements, such as clip art or WordArt.

6-3

Decision: (Select one of the following options.)

☐ **One version of flyer**
   Justification: _____

   _____

   _____

   _____

☐ **Multiple versions of flyer**
   Version 1: Audience: _____

              Justification: _____

              _____

              _____

              _____

              _____

   Version 2: Audience: _____

              Justification: _____

              _____

              _____

              _____

              _____

   Version 3: Audience: _____

              Justification: _____

              _____

              _____

              _____

              _____

Determine the content of the flyer(s).
(Use information from the invitation—6-1.)

_____

_____

_____

Format the flyer(s).

6-4

Prepare Newsletter

- Create an appealing design

- Incorporate previously prepared materials

- Key from handwritten source copy

- Edit and finalize team-written articles using comments and track changes

- Condense an article to fit space available

- Abstract material from other sources

The Grand Opening Committee recommended that a newsletter be developed and sent out to a wide variety of individuals who have an interest in The Sports Connection. Ms. McKay agreed with the recommendation. The Grand Opening Committee suggested using the logo and the banner heading, *The Sports Connection News and Views,* for the first issue. The committee suggested that you might want to include a contest to get readers involved in naming the newsletter.

Ms. McKay asked you to serve as editor and put together a comprehensive newsletter that will be sent to the following groups:

- Users and potential users of The Sports Connection

- Volunteers and potential volunteers

- Corporate sponsors and potential sponsors

- Advisory Council

The newsletter contains a variety of short articles—some of which have been provided by other individuals, some of which you have already prepared, and some of which you will create. Include the news items listed below. Delete any instructions contained in the data files provided. If you wish to do so, you may modify the format used in these files.

1. Mission of The Sports Connection (see *Welcome to The Sports Connection,* pages viii–x).

2. Message from the director (handwritten copy, page 88).

3. Description of the role of the Advisory Council.
   - See the Word file **Advisory Council** from the data files plus points selected from the opening of the simulation, page 88.
   - Directory of council members (from the directory you prepared in Job 4-5).

4. Articles on the importance of volunteers and corporate sponsorships (**Newsletter Articles** Word file from the data files). Review revisions and comments; then finalize articles.

Comments
Insert, Comment
Reviewing Toolbar
View, Toolbars,
Reviewing

Advisory Council

Newsletter Articles

S O F T W A R E

Document Properties
File, Properties,
Statistics Tab
Word Count
Tools, Word Count

Contest

Logo

5. Condensed version of the newspaper article (from Job 6-2). Summarize the article so that it will be approximately one-third the length of the original article (about 180 words). Use Document Properties or the Word Count function to aid you.

6. Fee schedule (see Job 2-4). Add an introductory statement indicating that the fees were determined by the Advisory Council and be sure to include the statement from the gift criteria specifying no fees for the financially disadvantaged.

7. Invite readers to submit a name for the newsletter to you. The winner will be selected by the Advisory Council and will receive a prize of athletic apparel and equipment valued at $125. Include procedures for submitting suggestions (Word file **Contest** from the data files).

You may experiment with the format of this initial issue. Include the company logo (Word file **Logo** from the data files) with the name of the newsletter. Use columns, clip art, WordArt, lines, charts, or other design features to make the newsletter interesting and attractive. Create side headings for each article. Format the side headings with a drop cap.

Try to fit Items 1 through 5 on pages 1 and 2 using equal size columns. Format page 3 as one column with Item 6 on the top half and Item 7 on the bottom half of the page. Use a divider line between the items.

C R I T I C A L T H I N K I N G

Team Documents

MANY DIFFERENT procedures are used in business settings to complete documents as a team. In Project 6, your team used these strategies for completing documents:
- The team agrees on and provides the specific information to be included and selects a sample document for the preferred format. An individual then completes the job (Job 6-1).
- The team provides only a broad outline of topics to include in the article. An individual is responsible for providing the specific information and formatting it appropriately (Job 6-2).
- The content, the strategy, and the preparation of the document are completed by an individual team member. The only role of the team is in determining that the document is needed (Job 6-3).
- The team members participate in the writing and editing by using the track changes features of Microsoft Word software (Job 6-4).

1. Which approach is most effective for a team to use in preparing documents?
2. When a team makes specific suggestions to an individual for preparing a document, what latitude does the individual preparing the document have in making changes in the team's suggestions?
3. Is it possible to function effectively as a team when individual members are in different locations?

6-4

Message from....

The Sports Connection

Thanks to the generous donation of a wonderful community-minded philanthropist and the tremendous support of our city officials, corporate sponsors, volunteers, and staff, The Sports Connection is now a reality. All of the major construction work has been completed, and the final inspection is scheduled for April 4.

The Grand Opening Committee encourages you and your family and friends to be a part of the exciting Grand Opening Celebration on Saturday, April 15. The dedication ceremony begins at 10:00 in the morning with the Mayor declaring April 15 as Sports Connection Day and the Community Foundation President presenting the key to The Sports Connection facility to us. At the conclusion of the program, the official party will lead the tour of the facilities. Our volunteers will be available to conduct tours throughout the afternoon. A number of exhibitions featuring several coaches from Central University, some of our volunteer coaches, and some of our participants are scheduled as part of the tour.

The picnic lunch will be served in the recreation area beginning at 11:30. The gymnasium has been designated as the alternate site in the event of rain. Many of our corporate sponsors generously contributed to the luncheon and also donated prizes that will be given throughout the event.

Some of the activities of The Sports Connection have already begun; others will begin after the final inspection of the facilities. A complete schedule of the activities that are now available is posted at The Sports Connection office. Participants are encouraged to sign up early. As events fill, new ones will be opened as long as volunteer coaches and facilities are available. Forms are available for users to suggest additional activities that would be of interest.

—Karen McKay, Director

6-5 Optional Internet Activities: New Orleans

- Locate and compile information from Web sites
- Locate and print map
- Determine distance using maps
- Locate hotel and flight information

Task 1: Map to The Sports Connection

Use one of the map features available on the Internet to print a map of the area in which The Sports Connection is located. This map will be faxed or mailed to individuals who inquire about the location of The Sports Connection.

One source for a map is **http://www.mapquest.com**. Locate the address 5600 St. Charles Avenue, New Orleans, Louisiana.

Task 2: Fitness Centers in New Orleans

Ms. McKay has asked you to determine whether you can locate information about fitness centers that are available in New Orleans. She particularly wants to know if any appeal directly to youth and are very low cost centers that might compete with The Sports Connection activities. She suggested that you use the Internet to find this information. Use *fitness and health* or *Fitness Centers New Orleans* as key words for the search. Check to see if any of the centers you find have a Web page; if so, go to the Web page and review the available information so that you can brief Ms. McKay on what's available.

Task 3: Making Travel Arrangements

Ms. McKay has been invited to visit the JR Sports Center located at 2150 North Stemmons Freeway in Dallas, Texas. Use Mapquest.com or another map site to do the following:

- Find out the approximate driving distance and time from The Sports Connection to Dallas. If the driving time is less than eight hours, she will consider driving. Use the maps available on the Internet to determine this information.

- She also wants you to find the name, address, telephone number, and fax number of a nice hotel very close to the JR Sports Center.

- If the driving time is more than eight hours, you should also check flight schedules to determine what is available. She plans to leave on a Thursday morning and return on late Friday afternoon or evening if she flies. If she drives, she will leave on Saturday morning.

© GETTY IMAGES/PHOTODISC

scenario

The Grand Opening of The Sports Connection was a huge success and created a lot of interest in The Sports Connection. Both users and volunteers are eager to get involved. Ms. McKay asked you to invite the planners of the Grand Opening to a victory celebration to thank them personally. She also asked you to update the database of volunteers you created earlier (Job 4-2) and to manage all communications with users of The Sports Connection. You will create a database of users so that you can use subsets to merge with form letters about various Sports Connection activities.

profile

Communicating

project

7

7-1 Prepare Merge Letter and Envelopes

- Finalize the rough draft
- Use Mail Merge to prepare personalized letters and envelopes
- Use Outlook Contacts list

The rough-draft letter shown at the right needs to be finalized and set up as a main document for a mail merge. The letter will be sent to The Sports Connection Advisory Council and the Grand Opening Committee.

Letterhead

Task 1: Merge Main Document with Outlook Advisory Council Contacts List

Prepare the form letters for the Advisory Council from the Contacts list of Microsoft Outlook. (If you have not completed pp. 139–140 in the Software Training Manual, please do so now.)

In Outlook, open the Advisory Council Contacts list and complete the mail merge process. Insert **Letterhead** from the data files. Then key the letter, making the changes noted. Date the letter April 18. Choose the appropriate fields to personalize the letters. Both you and Ms. McKay have worked extensively with these two groups and are on a first name basis with all of them. Therefore, use the first name field for the salutation. Print the form letters.

Prepare the envelopes by using the Mail Merge feature in Word. As the data source, choose *Select from Outlook Contacts* and select the *Advisory Council* folder.

Task 2: Merge Main Document with Grand Opening Committee Data File

Note

The data file can be created in Word, Excel, or Access. You could also create a new Contacts folder for the data.

To prepare the mail merge for the Grand Opening Committee, you will need to create a data file named **Grand Opening Committee-data**. See Job 5-5 for the complete names and job titles for the three employees on the committee: Mr. Khoo, Ms. Hinnant, and Mr. Kihlken. Use The Sports Connection address for these employees.

Because the data source is different in Task 2, you cannot use the same main document. However, you may copy the body of the letter and closing from the main document prepared in Task 1. (*Hint:* Edit the letter appropriately for the Grand Opening Committee.) Follow the same procedures as above, inserting the letterhead file and inserting appropriate fields.

Prepare the envelopes using mail merge in Word.

7-1

Dear

Thanks to the efforts of a wonderful, dedicated team the Grand Opening ^of The Sports Connection was a ~~big~~ huge

success. The turnout ~~for~~ for the event ~~for~~ far exceeded our most ambitious

expectations. Perhaps the ~~very~~ most important result ~~of the event~~ is the

tremendous interest the event created in the activities of the sports

connection. More than a hundred potential users and volunteers have called

The ~~Sports Connection~~ office to request information about becoming involved in the

activities of The Sports Connection.

I appreciate the excellent work you did as a member of (the Grand Opening

Committee/The Sports Connection Advisory Council). Would you and your guest

join us for an informal victory celebration barbecue at my home at 2476 Broadway on Friday

evening, May 5, at 7:30? The staff of The Sports Connection would like to thank

you personally for playing such a key role in the success of the Grand Opening.

Please call The Sports Connection office and let us know if you can join us for

a much-deserved evening of fellowship and relaxation. We hope you will be able to attend.

Sincerely

Karen McKay

Director

7-2

Update and Use Database

- Import an Excel table

- Create a new table

- Run queries

- Produce a form

You have a database that contains contact information about new volunteers who will help to coach various sports. You also have an Excel table of experienced volunteers who worked with the St. Charles Park and Recreation Center prior to the creation of The Sports Connection. You want to combine this information into one database and do some further work with that database.

Volunteers
Exp Volunteers

1. Open the Access file **Volunteers** from the data files. Import the **Exp Volunteers** Excel file (use *File; Get External Data*) into the **Volunteers** database as a new table named *Experienced Volunteers*.

2. Query the *Experienced Volunteers* table to produce a list containing the first and last names of experienced volunteers who coach the following Sport Codes: 2, 12, 14, 1, 13. Sort the list by Sport Code. Name the query *Experienced Volunteers by Sport*.

3. Query the *New Volunteers* table to produce a list containing the first and last names of new volunteers who coach the following Sport Codes: 2, 12, 14, 1, 13. Sort the list by Sport Code. Name the query *New Volunteers by Sport*.

4. Set up a table of sports offered by The Sports Connection. Use the following columns: *ID, Sport,* and *Type. Type* refers to whether a sport is Co-ed, Girls, or Boys. Use a separate ID number for each sport type. Sports offered include aerobics (co-ed), baseball (boys), basketball (boys and girls), dance (co-ed), educational programs (co-ed, boys, and girls), golf (co-ed), soccer (boys and girls), softball (girls), swimming (co-ed), tennis (boys and girls) and volleyball (boys and girls). Name the table *Sports*.

5. Create a copy of the *New Volunteers* table. Name the copy *All Volunteers*. Copy all of the records from the *Experienced Volunteers* table and paste them into the *All Volunteers* table. Add a new field at the beginning of the table named *New ID* and set data type to *AutoNumber;* then delete the old ID field. Adjust column sizes so that the entire table can be printed on one page in landscape view. Print the table.

6. Sort the *All Volunteers* table in ascending order by the Last Name field. Create a form containing the First Name, Last Name, Home Phone, and Business Phone fields from the *All Volunteers* table. Use the Standard columnar format. Name the form *Telephone List—Volunteers*.

7. Use the information to create a table containing the May schedule of activities for The Sports Connection. Name the table *May Schedule*. Use the *Medium Time* format for the Time field. Sort the table in ascending order by the Sport Code field.

7-2

May Schedule

Sport Code	Sport	Type	Days	Time	Coach	Age Group
2	Baseball	Boys	MW	3:30	Bruce Leski	15 or younger
2	Baseball	Boys	TT	5:30	Bill McGee	16 or older
12	Softball	Girls	MW	5:30	Kathy Voris	16 or older
12	Softball	Girls	TT	3:30	Laura Popal	15 or younger
14	Tennis	Boys	MW	3:30	Kim Ryan	15 or younger
14	Tennis	Boys	MW	5:30	Dan Sadik	16 or older
15	Tennis	Girls	TT	3:30	Central Univ.	15 or younger
15	Tennis	Girls	TT	5:30	Central Univ.	16 or older
1	Aerobics	Co-ed	MW	4:00	Ruth Pratt	15 or younger
1	Aerobics	Co-ed	TT	4:00	Steve Wuori	16 or older
13	Swimming	Co-ed	MW	3:30	Lu Lin	15 or younger
13	Swimming	Co-ed	TT	3:30	Anne Taber	16 or older

Create Database

- Create database

- Add fields to a database

Information about the first 25 users who signed up to participate in The Sports Connection is provided at the right. You have decided to create a **Users** database, and you will use this information to get the database set up properly. Then you will ask one of the office volunteers to enter the data for all the other users.

1. Create a database named **Users**, and enter the data about the first 25 users in a table named *Users.*

2. Add a field named *ID* to the *Users* table. Place the field before the First Name field. Use *AutoNumber* for the data type for the field.

3. Add a field named *Title* to the *Users* table. Place the field before the First Name field. Enter *Mr.* or *Ms.* in the field based on the person's gender.

CRITICAL THINKING

Analyze Databases

Ms. McKay has asked you to analyze The Sports Connection databases and make suggestions for improving their structure or use.

1. Review all the categories of information in the **Volunteers** database (Job 7-2) and decide if additional fields would be important to add to the **Users** database (Job 7-3). Make a list of additional fields to discuss with Ms. McKay. Write a short justification for the addition of any fields.
2. What relationships might you want to consider between the **Volunteers** database and the **Users** database? Describe these relationships so that you can discuss them with Ms. McKay.
3. The *May Schedule* table in the **Volunteers** database does not have a primary key assigned. You are considering adding a field named *Section* after the Sport Code field and using a multiple-field primary key. You are also considering placing all of the tables from the **Users** database and the **Volunteers** database in the same database file. How would these changes help you relate data?

7-3

First & Last Name		Address	*City	Postal Code	Age	Gender
Lee	Bader	501 Norton Ave.	New Orleans	70123-1123	17	Male
Bill	Ayers	66 Stutz Dr.	New Orleans	70126-2226	21	Male
Gail	Barto	201 Taft Place	New Orleans	70119-3319	19	Female
Brian	Luke	345 Marion Ave.	Metairie	70005-2355	17	Male
Julia	Riley	2221 Nora St.	Metairie	70003-5533	16	Female
Ben	Mabry	448 Seine St.	New Orleans	70114-1114	19	Male
Ann	Patel	608 Pope St.	New Orleans	70121-0021	18	Female
Steve	Drury	558 Airline Hwy.	Kenner	70062-0062	20	Male
John	Reese	702 Elder St.	New Orleans	70122-2322	17	Male
Betty	Quinn	388 Eton St.	New Orleans	70114-1114	17	Female
Maria	Salvas	4409 Mandarin St.	Metairie	70005-0005	16	Female
David	Ryan	3389 Jefferson Blvd.	Kenner	70062-1162	20	Male
Jose	Mendez	4306 Jefferson Blvd.	Kenner	70062-3362	21	Male
Po-Ling	Wong	402 Utica St.	Metairie	70002-4622	18	Female
Paul	Fogle	88 Sage St.	New Orleans	70122-4322	19	Male
Te-Long	Wang	601 Toulon St.	New Orleans	70129-6629	18	Male
Boyd	Bell	2907 Poydras St.	New Orleans	70113-2213	16	Male
Ana	Garcia	4089 Slidell St.	New Orleans	70114-1314	17	Female
Phill	Asbill	2288 Clarke St.	Metairie	70002-0202	19	Male
Lesa	Berry	706 Georgia St.	Metairie	70005-3355	22	Female
Ramon	Arvay	3310 Flagler St.	Metairie	70003-1011	20	Male
Melvin	Norton	2206 Audubon Blvd.	New Orleans	70125-2206	18	Male
Anne	Pace	2766 Baronne St.	New Orleans	70113-3343	19	Female
Don	Pruitt	540 Basin St.	New Orleans	70112-4412	22	Male
Patsy	Phyall	806 Bourbon St.	New Orleans	70116-8806	21	Female

*Note: All cities are in Louisiana.

7-4 Prepare Memo and Print Labels from Database

- Prepare memo

- Print mailing labels from database

Karen McKay drafted the memo at the right to be sent to all registered users of The Sports Connection concerning the fee schedule the Advisory Council implemented at its last meeting.

1. Key the memo from Karen McKay, Director, using the Professional Memo template.

2. Expand the placeholder box for the company name so that *The Sports Connection* will fit on one line. Use this template for all of the memos you prepare for The Sports Connection.

3. Send a copy of the memo to the Advisory Council.

4. Attach the fee schedule created in Project 2 (2-4).

5. Use *Fee Structure* as the reference line.

6. Print mailing labels sorted by the Postal Code field from the **Users** database. Use *English* for the Unit of Measure and *Avery 6460, 1" x 2 5/8"* labels. Increase the font size to *12*.

SOFTWARE TIPS

Labels
Reports, New, Label Wizard; select Users table, follow the Wizard steps

7-4

Several users have asked questions about The Sports Connection fee schedule; therefore, I am providing each registered user of The Sports Connection with information about the process of setting fees and with a copy of the current fee schedule.

Criteria for the gift to establish The Sports Connection specified that the Advisory Council is responsible for overseeing the financial operation of The Sports Connection. This responsibility includes securing additional funds to enhance the operations and ensuring that young people who are financially disadvantaged (as determined by the Community Foundation Guidelines) have access to all activities of The Sports Connection at no charge. Community Foundation Guidelines are posted in the office and are also available directly from the Community Foundation.

The Sports Connection Advisory Council has established the following guides for fees:

- Financially disadvantaged youth receive passes that provide complete access, and they pay no fees whatsoever.

- Fees are not charged for use of the park; the soccer, baseball, and softball fields; the basketball, volleyball, and tennis courts; aerobics and dance classes; or for educational programs.

- Fees will be charged for access passes to the swimming pool, driving range, locker rooms, and to the equipment in the fitness center.

- Fees may be paid for access passes on a daily, weekly, or monthly basis. Passes are available for individual activities or at a reduced rate for access to all activities.

- The Sports Connection Advisory Council reviews fees and may change them at its Fall meeting.

Attachment: Fee schedule

Design Announcement and Print Labels from Query

- Design an announcement
- Query database
- Print labels from query

Use the information at the right to prepare an announcement of an upcoming Junior Golf Clinic. Spell out all abbreviations. The clinic is designed to introduce young girls and boys to the basics of golf. The Sports Connection is making a conscious effort to get more girls involved in sports, especially golf and tennis. Announcements of events are usually formatted similar to the illustration shown below. Use clip art that would be appropriate for golf. You may also want to include clip art of an eagle if you have one available, since the coaches of the Central University Eagles are presenting the clinic.

Query The Sports Connection **Users** database to obtain a list of all users who are under 18 years old. Sort by postal code. Print mailing labels for the individuals on the list.

Tennis Exhibition

What:	The Tennis Exhibition is a special event designed to help you improve your tennis game and enjoy playing tennis more.
When:	Monday evening, April 1, from 6:00–8:00
Where:	The Sports Connection tennis courts
General Information:	Registration is not required. The program includes: • a discussion on conditioning • a demonstration of key techniques • an exhibition match
Presented by:	Paul Sanchez, Tennis Pro Running Fox Tennis and Golf Club Christi Daniels, Tennis Pro Lakeside Tennis and Golf Club

7-5

What: The Junior Golf Clinic is a special event for girls and boys who are 17 years old or younger who would like to learn how to play golf.

When: Sat. morn, April 6, from 8:30-11:30

Where: The S C Practice Putting and Driving Range

General Information: Call The S C office (555-0139) to register no later than Th, April 5, at 4:30 p.m. No prior golf knowledge is required. Golf clubs will be provided if you do not own golf clubs. Golf access passes are not required for this special event.

Young girls are especially encouraged to learn to play golf. Many business contacts are made on golf courses. In addition to being fun, golf provides an excellent opportunity to network with managers, customers, and clients. Informal networking is a key way to enhance your career.

Presented by: Women and Men's Golf Coaches and Teams Central University Eagles

7-6 Develop Handouts and Labels

- Prepare handouts for seminar for fitness and aerobics classes

- Search the Internet

- Summarize information

- Query database and print labels sorted by gender and in alphabetical order

1. Prepare a handout entitled *Enjoy a Healthy Lifestyle.* This handout will be used during a fitness seminar that will be offered to all The Sports Connection users. The seminar will include breakout sessions for male and female users.

WordArt
Click button on the Drawing toolbar

   - Use WordArt for the title. You may also use appropriate photos or clip art if you wish to do so.
   - Key the information at the right and format the document using a one-column format. Format headings appropriately. You may use Drop Caps or other design elements to enhance the document and make it more interesting for a seminar handout.

2. Select one of the major topics or subtopics discussed in the handout you prepared and use the Internet to find additional information about the topic. Coordinate with your class so that all of the major topics are selected and researched. Use a key word search to find needed information. Examples of key words are *fitness, health and sports, exercise, nutrition, aerobics, smoking,* and *diet.*
   - Prepare a summary of the information you found.
   - Use the same format as you used for the handout you prepared.
   - Prepare a list of the sources for the information you used.

3. Query the **User** database for a listing of all male users of The Sports Connection. Sort the list by alphabetical order and print file folder labels (Avery Index Maker 3 Tab) for handouts used in the breakout session.

4. Query the **User** database for a listing of all female users of The Sports Connection. Sort the list by alphabetical order and print file folder labels (Avery Index Maker 3 Tab) for handouts used in the breakout session.

7-6

Although young people are more likely to die or be severely injured in automobile or work accidents and violent assaults involving alcohol or drugs than from illnesses, living a healthy lifestyle is still very important. It is important for young people because living a healthy lifestyle is the key to looking, feeling, and doing your best.

What is a Healthy Lifestyle?

Living a healthy lifestyle does not mean giving up everything that is fun. It does mean that you must make wise choices in a variety of areas including diet, weight control, exercise, use of tobacco, alcohol, and drugs, and taking preventive measures to avoid accidents and diseases. Physical fitness results from living a healthy lifestyle.

Fitness Evaluation

The Sports Connection has arranged to make a comprehensive fitness evaluation available to users of the Fitness Center and aerobics classes. Graduate and undergraduate student interns in the Exercise Science Department of Central University can administer an evaluation of your current fitness level for a nominal fee of $20. The evaluation includes:

• Resting heart rate and blood pressure
• Height, weight, and body (fat) composition
• Flexibility
• Muscular strength and endurance
• Cardiorespiratory fitness
• Cholesterol screening
• Dietary analysis
• Nutritional counseling
• Personalized exercise program

Comparable evaluations at local health clubs cost $50 to $100. The program is supervised by Dr. Lynn Massa, head of the Exercise Science Department.

Diet and Weight Control

A healthy diet refers to both the selection and the quantity of food. A low fat, low sodium, low sugar diet is ideal. For most young people, the best advice is to eat a variety of foods including vegetables, fruits, and grain products. Studies show that more than 20 percent of teenage boys and girls are overweight. A small, but growing percentage of teenage girls with a desire to be extremely thin develop severe eating disorders such as anorexia nervosa or bulimia nervosa. Excessive dieting and exercise lead to major health and emotional problems.

Exercise

An appropriate exercise program is critical for physical fitness. To be effective, an exercise program must include a cardiovascular workout as well as muscular strength and endurance workouts. A good workout should include at least 20 minutes of exercise three times a week. Combining a good exercise program and a healthy diet provides effective weight control.

Smoking, Alcohol, and Drugs

Smoking, alcohol, and illegal drugs have severe health consequences as well as severe consequences on physical performance. In some cases, athletes foolishly take drugs (amphetamines and steroids) to enhance performance for a period of time, but they do irreparable harm to their health.

Preventive Measures

A healthy lifestyle requires preventive as well as proactive measures. Driving is a good example of an area where preventive measures are extremely important since accidents are a primary cause of deaths of young people.

7-7

Merge Letter with Database

Letterhead

- Prepare mail merge letter and envelopes for volunteer coaches

- Drag database information and drop into Word document

The rough-draft letter shown at the right needs to be finalized and set up as a main document for a mail merge. The letter will be sent to all new and experienced volunteers who coach aerobics, baseball, softball, swimming, or tennis.

1. Key the letter at the right, making the changes noted. Adjust the font size so that the letter will fit on one page. Insert the **Letterhead** file at the top of the page.

2. Set up the necessary fields to personalize the letters. Use first names for the salutation. Date the letter April 20.

3. Drag the *May Schedule* table from the **Volunteers** database and drop it in the letter where noted.
   - To drag the table, open both the Access database and the Word document. Size the windows so that both the Access database window and part of the Word document are displayed on the screen.
   - Click the *May Schedule* table icon in the Access database window and drag the icon to the Microsoft Word document. Release the mouse button.
   - Position the table at the appropriate place in the document, if needed.

4. Query the database for all volunteers who coach aerobics, baseball, softball, swimming, and tennis (use the Sport Code field to enter criteria). The query results should include all fields needed to prepare letters to these volunteers.

5. Merge the letter with the volunteers who coach aerobics, baseball, softball, swimming, and tennis.

Optional: Prepare envelopes for the letters.

7-7

Dear

    Most of you know that The Sports Connection Advisory Council approved
baseball,
aerobics, softball, tennis, and swimming as the sports to be offered in may.
                    is
The May schedule shown below.

                (Drop schedule here)
                    could
    This limited schedule ~~will~~ be expanded significantly if additional
                                                 Normally,
volunteers step forward to coach teams in the various sports. A primary and a
                  available
backup coach must be ~~named~~ before a team can be added to the schedule. User
demand exceeds availability in all sports. If you or if you know of anyone who
would be willing to coach one of the sports offered in May, please call The
                                      within one week
Sports Connection office and share that information with us.

    We appreciate the tremendous contributions that all of our volunteers make
to The Sports Connection programs. Without our volunteers, our offerings would
   much
be more limited.

Sincerely

Student's name

Assistant Director

xx

*However, we are
not adhering to
that guideline
for the May
schedule since*

Optional Internet Activity: Corporate Sponsors

• Compile information from Web sites

Ms. McKay asked you to compile a list of some of the major corporate partners that sponsor collegiate sports. Use a search engine to find addresses for the following Web sites. Access these sites to obtain that information:

SEC Sports
Big South Conference
Atlantic Coast Conference
Big Ten Conference
PAC-10 Conference

For additional sites, search for *Conferences* on the NCAA (National Collegiate Athletic Association) Web site.

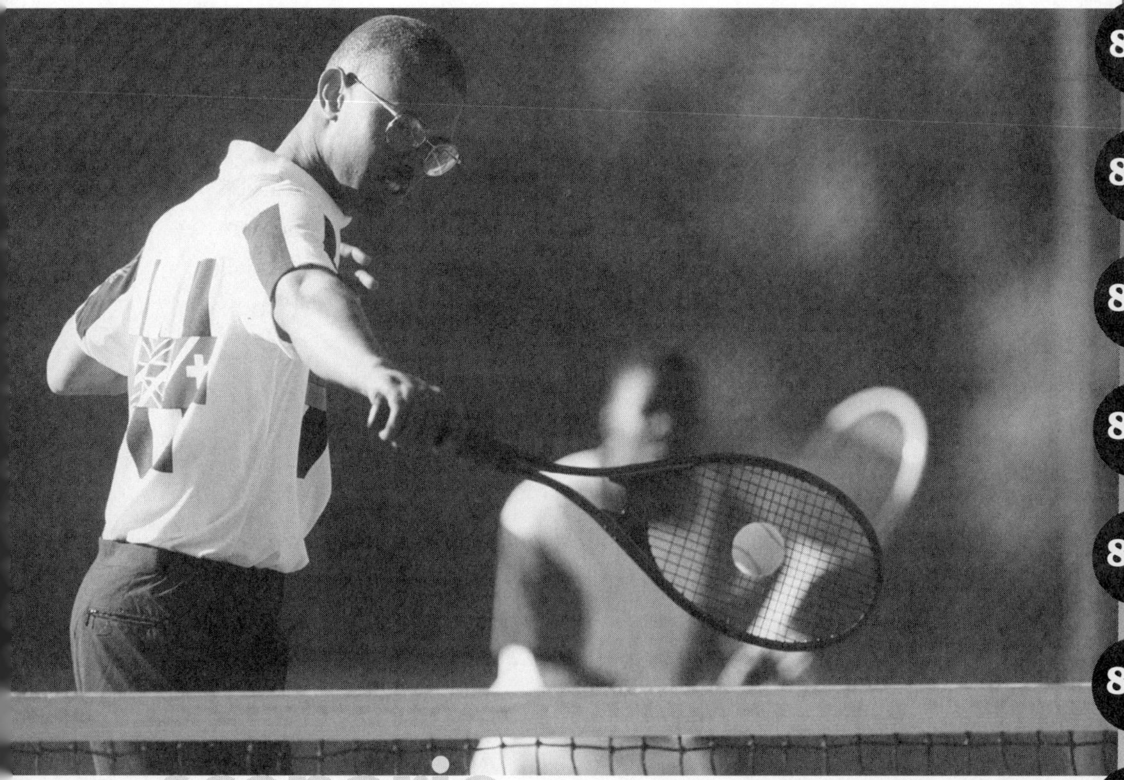

© GETTY IMAGES/PHOTODISC

8-1 Design application form

8-2 Research topic and prepare presentation

8-3 Manage files

8-4 Prepare employment announcement for Web

8-5 Compose memo for Web

8-6 Reformat document for Web

8-7 Select standard theme for documents

8-8 Optional Internet activity

scenario

The Sports Connection is now operational and progress is being made in making the operation efficient. Managing information and communicating effectively with users and volunteers is a major challenge. Therefore, you have decided to begin putting information on the Web and also to use the intranet as a tool of communication.

profile

project

Managing Information

8

8-1

Logo

Design Application Form

- Design and prepare application form

The Sports Connection needs to have an attractive application form that can be placed in local schools and businesses for prospective users to pick up and complete. The information at the right must be included on the form. The users will handwrite the information on the form, but the form should be designed so that it is easy to enter the data from the form into the **Users** database.

1. Format the form using .5″ top margin and .75″ side margins so that the form will fit on one page.

2. Insert The Sports Connection logo at the upper left corner. Use WordArt for the name *The Sports Connection* at the top of the page to the right of the logo. Use WordArt to center the address and telephone number below the name in a smaller text size than the name.

3. Center the title *Membership Application*, and use solid shading to separate the heading and the application information. Use text boxes or paragraph borders for the information to be supplied in this area.

4. Use regular type and solid shading for the *Payment Plan* section. Include the information about the payment plan shown at the right. Use table format for the information.

5. Use regular type and solid shading for the *Participation Estimate* section. Include the information about the participation estimate shown at the right.

6. Use table format for the information about the sports and the frequency of participation. List the sports in two columns so that the form will fit on one page.

A sample form is illustrated below to provide ideas. Your form may vary from the one illustrated.

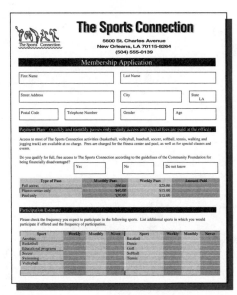

8-1

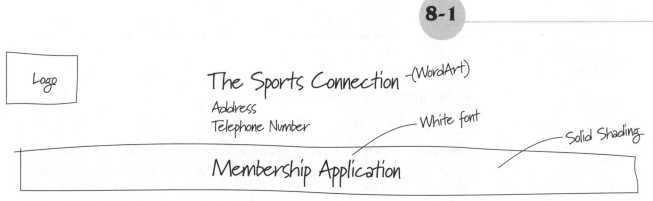

The Sports Connection —(WordArt)
Address
Telephone Number — White font
Solid Shading

Membership Application

User information required:

First Name	Last Name		
Street Address	City	State LA	
Postal Code	Telephone Number	Gender	Age

Payment Plan (weekly and monthly passes only—daily access and special fees are paid at the office)

Access to most of The Sports Connection activities (basketball, volleyball, baseball, soccer, softball, tennis, walking and jogging track) are available at no charge. Fees are charged for the fitness center and pool, as well as for special classes and events.

Do you qualify for full, free access to The Sports Connection according to the guidelines of the Community Foundation for being financially disadvantaged?   Yes   No   Do not know

Type of Pass	Monthly Pass	Weekly Pass	Amount Paid
Full access	$60.00	$25.00	
Fitness center only	$40.00	$15.00	
Pool only	$30.00	$12.00	

Shade

Participation Estimate:
Please check the frequency you expect to participate in the following sports. List additional sports in which you would participate if offered and the frequency of participation.

[List the 11 sports in the first column; do not separate by gender; provide 3 more column heads—Weekly, Monthly, and Never; leave columns blank for user to check. Leave blank rows for 3—5 sports to be added.]

8-2 Research Topic and Prepare Presentation

- Research topic

- Prepare PowerPoint presentation

- Option: post on Web

The Sports Connection recently created a Web site. Each week a presentation providing tips on a particular sport or on improving performance is featured on the Web site.

Your task is to:

1. Select a sport that you would like to learn more about.

2. Use the Internet to research ways to improve performance in that sport. Obtain information from a minimum of three different sources.

3. Use Word's thesaurus to help you find creative words for your presentation.

4. Prepare a PowerPoint presentation to provide tips on improving performance in that particular sport. Select the template you prefer or modify a template to provide the appearance you would like for your presentation. Prepare at least six slides.

Optional: Publish the presentation on the Web.

Manage Files

- Create a new folder

- Add documents to folder

The Sports Connection needs to organize all of the information about the various sports; therefore, create a folder to accomplish this task.

1. Name the folder *Sports Tips.*

2. Place your PowerPoint presentation that you prepared in Job 8-2 in the folder.

3. You anticipate that the sports tips will generate additional interest in the activities of The Sports Connection. Therefore, place the new member application form you created in Job 8-1 in this folder so that it will be available when anyone shows an interest in becoming a member.

Team Project Option:

Obtain presentations prepared by six or more of your classmates and add them to the folder. Organize the presentations by sport. Use one of the following alternatives to obtain the presentations:

- If you have e-mail available, have your classmates mail the presentation to you as an attachment to the e-mail.

- If you have a network, have the presentations stored on a common drive that everyone can access.

- Copy the presentation to a CD and copy it to your system so that you can add it to your folder.

8-4

Prepare Employment Announcement for Web

SC Information
Logo

- Use a Web page template

- Link to another Web page

- Option: post on intranet

The Sports Connection has created a new position and wants to post it on the Web. Use the Web page template in Word to prepare an employment announcement for the new position of Sports Coordinator. (*Option:* Use FrontPage or another Web page creation program.) You will link the Employment Page on the Web to the Web page (**SC Information** from the data files) that provides information about The Sports Connection.

1. Select a color for the main heading, *Employment,* and for the headings above bulleted points.

2. Place the information at the right on the Web page.

3. Place a hyperlink before *E-Mail* under the *Apply* section. Use the filename **SC Information** for the hyperlink and link to the file so that potential applicants can get additional information about The Sports Connection.

4. Place The Sports Connection logo at the top of the page. (Use **Logo** from the data files.) Add other design elements as desired to make an attractive page.

5. Save the file as a single file Web page named **Employment**. Use *The Sports Connection Employment* as the page title.

Optional: Post on the intranet.

8-4

Employment

The Sports Connection has a full-time position available for a Sports Coordinator. The Sports Coordinator is responsible for scheduling and coordinating all sports programs as well as managing all volunteer coaches and conducting basic training for volunteers. Some evening work is required.

Skills and Knowledge Required

- Basic knowledge of all sports offered.

- Ability to communicate effectively.

- Ability to build teams and lead them effectively.

Educational and Experience Requirements

- BS degree or AA degree with two years experience; prefer recreation or sports-related major.

- Two years work experience in coaching or supervising recreational activities preferred.

Apply

(Insert hyperlink)E-Mail: Send resume to director@sportsconnection.org

8-5

Compose Memo for Web

- Compose memo

- Option: post on intranet

Use the information at the right to compose a memo that you plan to post on the Web.

1. Use the Professional Memo template.

2. Address the memo to *The Sports Connection Users* from you.

3. Send a copy of the memo to Karen McKay. Date the memo June 6. Select an appropriate subject line.

4. Select *Web Page Preview* from the File menu to view the document as a Web page. Make adjustments to the document format to create an attractive Web page.

5. Save the file as a single file Web page named **Golf Memo June 6**. Use *Golf Opportunity* as the page title.

Optional: Post on the intranet.

CRITICAL THINKING

The Sports Connection Website

YOU HAVE created several documents that can be posted on The Sports Connection intranet or Web site. Think about how the intranet (for employee and volunteer use) and the Web site (for public use) could be improved.

1. What types of information (that would be helpful to employees and volunteers) could be placed on the intranet or Web site?
2. What types of information or forms to complete online (that would be helpful to users) could be placed on the Web site?
3. List three or four general criteria that should be considered in updating or planning a Web site.

8-5

A major corporate sponsor has made it possible for users of The Sports Connection to play golf at a local course. Use the information below to compose the memo to all users.

Course	River Course
Golf club	Sunnyside Golf Club
Days	Mondays through Thursdays
Time	8:00 a.m. to 1:00 p.m.
Cost	Nominal charge of $12 per person
Free access users	Six free passes available per day—a priority system has been developed to ensure that all eligible users have an opportunity to play golf

Reformat Document for Web

- Reformat an article from a newsletter prepared earlier to use as a Web document

- Option: post on intranet

You will use an article (from Job 6-2) that you prepared for a newsletter earlier as a document in an online publication of The Sports Connection.

1. Remove all WordArt from the article. Format the title in the same font as the remainder of the article. Use bold.

2. Below the title add *By* and your name.

3. Reformat the article using single spacing and block paragraphs.

4. Select *Web Page Preview* from the File menu to view the document as a Web page. Make adjustments to the document format or add design elements to create an attractive Web page.

5. Save the file as a single file Web page named **Participate in Sports**. Use *Participate in Sports* as the page title.

Optional: Post on the intranet.

Select Standard Theme for Documents

- Evaluate themes and make a decision

- Apply a standard theme

Ms. McKay has asked you to review five themes that have been selected by the office staff, to recommend one theme that can be used for e-mail, and to standardize all documents that are posted on the Web.

Evaluate the following themes selected:

To view themes:
Format, Theme

- Blends

- Eclipse

- Expedition

- Level

- Radial

To evaluate the themes, you have decided to apply each theme to the same documents to compare the look of each. Use the documents you created in the following jobs to save time:

Job 8-4, Job 8-5, Job 8-6, and any e-mail message

Decide the theme that you will recommend. Prepare an e-mail to Ms. McKay indicating the theme you recommend and why you selected it. Apply the theme to the e-mail you prepare.

8-8

Optional Internet Activity: Careers in Sports

- Research topic

- Prepare and evaluate list of Web sites

A number of The Sports Connection users have begun to ask you for information about careers in sports. You have decided to prepare a list of sources to help users get information on the topic.

Use an Internet search engine to find Web sites with information about sports careers. Locate a list of different categories of sports careers. Then try to find information sources on as many of the categories as you can.

Prepare a list of Web sites that users can access to get information on sports careers. Check out each of the sources and use your own ranking system to evaluate them for the users. You might use descriptive terms such as *excellent, very helpful,* and *helpful.* Delete any references that are not helpful from your list.

Software Training Manual

contents

Microsoft Outlook 2003

Microsoft Outlook 2003

You will help Karen McKay, director of The Sports Connection, stay organized by using Microsoft Outlook 2003. Outlook is designed to help you manage messages, appointments, and contacts, and keep track of your activities. Take a few minutes to complete this training module on the Calendar, Contacts, and Tasks features of Outlook.

OPEN MICROSOFT OUTLOOK

Click *Start, All Programs, Microsoft Office, Microsoft Outlook 2003*. The Outlook Today screen will appear. The Navigation pane at the left of the screen includes options and folders you can use.

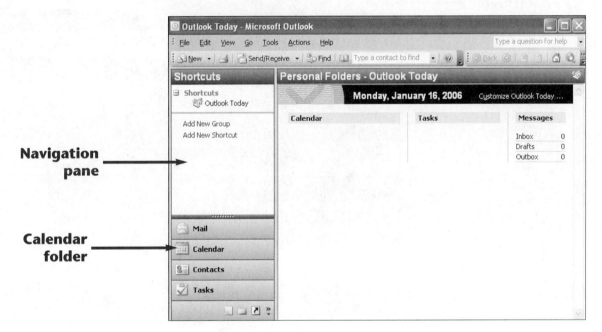

CALENDAR

The Calendar feature is used to schedule and keep track of appointments.

Schedule Appointments

1. Click *Calendar* in the Navigation pane.

2. Click the monthly scroll arrows to scroll to January of the current year. Then click *23* on the January calendar.

3. Click the *New Appointment* button on the Standard toolbar.

New Appointment button

Monthly scroll arrows

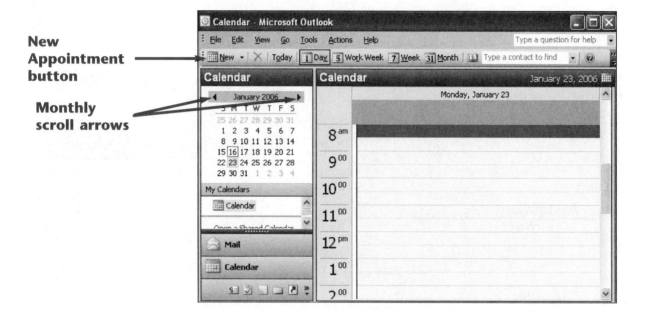

4. The Appointment dialog box displays. The top portion of the box is shown below. On the *Appointment* tab, enter data to schedule the 1 p.m. appointment with Fitness Staff in Room 253. Click the arrow buttons to set the starting time of the meeting at 1 p.m. and the ending time at 2 p.m. (*Note:* Effective time managers set starting times and ending times for appointments.) The default setting is to remind Karen of meetings with a soft chime 15 minutes prior to each appointment. Set the Label as *Business*.

Save and Close button →

5. Click the *Save and Close* button to save and close this appointment and to return to the Calendar screen. (*Note:* If the current date is after January 23, a reminder will appear immediately after you save the entry. Click *Dismiss* to close the reminder.)

Insert Document File in Appointment

To ensure preparation for her appointments, Karen McKay asks that you attach any files that she should review prior to an appointment. Follow these steps to attach files to the appointment.

Fitness Staff Agenda

1. On the Calendar screen, double-click the appointment set with the Fitness Staff for 1 p.m. on January 23.

2. From the Insert menu, click *File* or click the *Insert File* button.

3. Browse the directories and click the desired file (**Fitness Staff Agenda** from the data files). Click *Insert.* The filename appears on the Appointment dialog box.

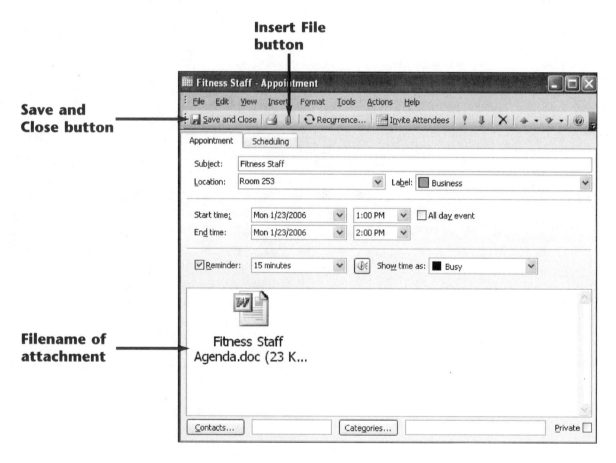

4. Click *Save and Close* to return to the Calendar screen.

Delete/Cancel Appointment

1. On the Calendar screen, click the appointment set on January 23 for the Fitness Staff.

2. Click the *Delete* button on the Standard toolbar to delete the appointment.

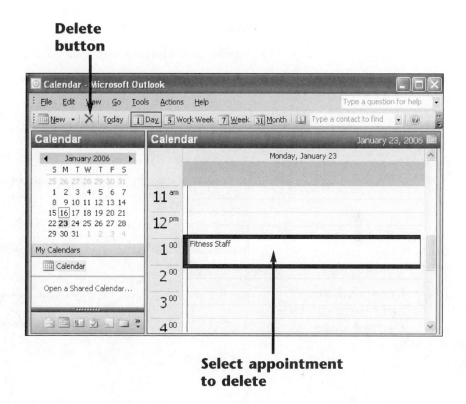

Delete button

Select appointment to delete

Practice

1. Add a 30-minute appointment with John Wilson in the Conference Room on January 30 at 1 p.m. Set the Label as *Business*.

2. Add an appointment for the Fitness Staff in the Conference Room on January 29 beginning at 9 a.m. and ending at 10 a.m. Attach the Fitness Staff Agenda file. Set the Label as *Business*.

3. Delete the appointment with John Wilson set on January 30.

4. Add an hour appointment with Wallace T. Brooks in Karen McKay's office on February 2 at 2 p.m. Set the Label as *Important*.

Move Appointment

Change time on same day:

1. On the Calendar screen, click the appointment set on January 29 at 9 a.m.

2. Drag appointment down to 3 p.m. and drop.

Change day of appointment:

1. Locate the appointment set on February 2 at 2 p.m.

2. Click the left border of the appointment. Drag the appointment to the monthly calendar and drop it on February 12.

   Note: To change to a different time, click *February 12* and drag appointment to correct time.

Drag and drop appointment to desired date

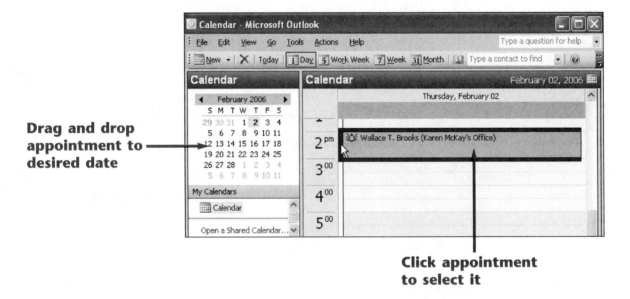

Click appointment to select it

Change Appointment to Recurring Appointment

1. On the Calendar screen, double-click the appointment on January 29 with the Fitness Staff. The Appointment dialog box appears.

2. Click the *Recurrence* button on the Standard toolbar.

Recurrence button

3. Make the following selections to schedule the Fitness Staff meeting for every Thursday at 3 p.m. beginning the week of January 29.
   a. Start time: 3 p.m.
   b. End time: 4 p.m.
   c. Recurrence pattern: Weekly on Thursday
   d. Range of recurrence: Start 1/29/20--. No end date.

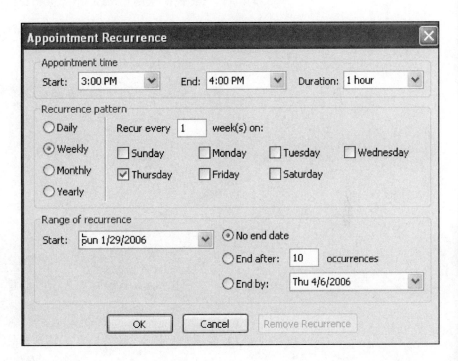

4. Click *OK* to save the settings. Click *Save and Close* to return to the Calendar screen.

Print Calendar

1. Access the Calendar screen, and go to the first Thursday in February of the current year. Click *File* on the menu bar. Click *Print.* The Print dialog box displays.

2. Select the appropriate printer from the *Name* box.

3. Under Print style, select *Daily Style.* Note the other print style options.

4. Under Print Range, select the date for the first Thursday in February for both the Start and End dates.

Page Setup button

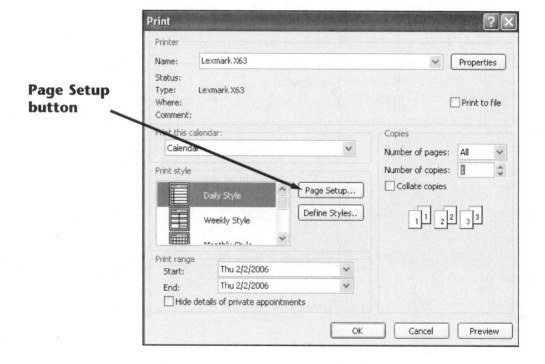

5. On the Print dialog box, click the *Page Setup* button to make changes to page setup. The following dialog box displays.

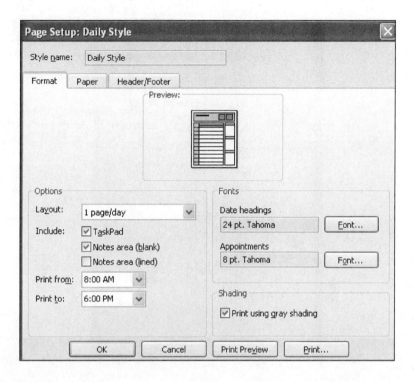

6. Under Options, choose:

   a. Layout for 1 page/day. Note another option is 2 pages/day. (The one page prints all on one page, whereas the two-page option prints the calendar on one page and tasks on the other page.)

   b. TaskPad (prints tasks on the TaskPad)

   c. Notes area (blank)

7. Under Print from, select *8:00 a.m.* Under Print to. select *6:00 p.m.*

8. Click the *Header/Footer* tab on the Page Setup dialog box. The following dialog box displays.

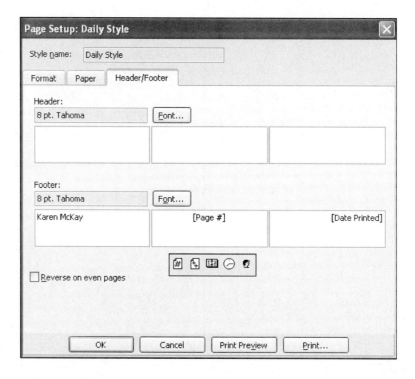

9. Under Footer, key *Karen McKay* in the left section of the footer. Leave the page number and the date in the center and right sections as shown. Click *OK*.

10. Click *OK* to print calendar.

Practice

Plans

1. Add a 30-minute appointment with Susan Walley in Karen McKay's office beginning at 10:30 p.m. on February 5. Set the Label as *Business*. Insert the document file **Plans** from the data files.

2. Locate the staff meeting to be held on the third Thursday in February. Change the starting time to 1 p.m. Edit the appointment to allow two hours for this meeting.

3. Move the 2 p.m. appointment with Wallace Brooks on February 12 to 1 p.m.

4. Print a weekly calendar for the week that contains February 12. Add a footer as shown above.

5. Print a daily calendar for February 5. Choose the two pages per day layout and add a footer as shown above.

TASKS

Enter Tasks

1. In the Outlook Navigation pane, click *Tasks*.

2. Click the *New Task* button on the Standard toolbar.

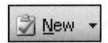

3. The following dialog box displays. For the Subject, key *New Fitness Staff Orientation*.

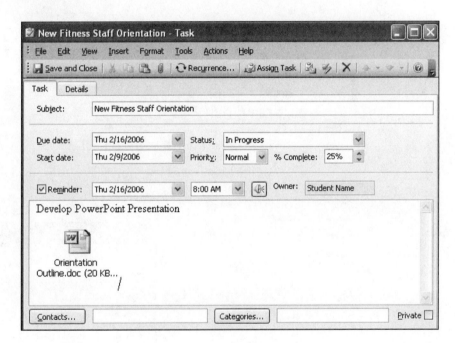

4. Select these options:

   a. Due date: Third Thursday in February

   b. Start date: Second Thursday in February

   c. Status: In Progress

   d. Priority: Normal

   e. % Complete: 25%

5. In the body, key this note that will help Ms. McKay in completing this task: *Develop PowerPoint Presentation*.

Orientation Outline

Insert a File

1. Position the insertion point in the body.

2. Click the *Insert File* button. Select the file to be inserted (**Orientation Outline** from the data files). Click *Insert*.

3. Click the *Save and Close* button.

Practice

Add a new task titled Celebrate Fitness Week; Due date: April 2 of next year; Start date: October 16 of current year; Status: In Progress; Priority: Normal; 0% Complete.

CONTACTS

The Contacts feature allows the user to maintain a list of contacts. To be useful, sub-folders are created so that different contacts lists can be maintained.

Create New Folder

1. Click *Contacts* in the Navigation pane.

2. Click *File* on the menu bar. Select *Folder,* then *New Folder*. The following Create New Folder dialog box displays.

3. Key *Advisory Council* in the Name box. Select *Contact Items* for the Folder contains option. Select *Contacts* as the place for the folder. Click *OK*.

Enter Contacts

1. In the Navigation pane, click *Folder List*.

2. Select the desired folder (Advisory Council).

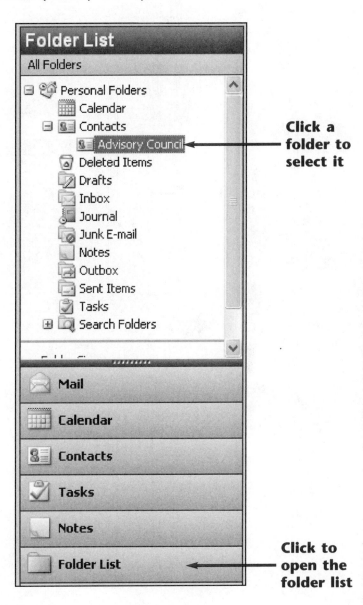

3. Click the *New Contact* button on the Standard toolbar.

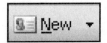

4. The Contact dialog box displays. Click the *General* tab. Add the following contact, as shown:

Full name:	Mr. Wallace T. Brooks
Job title:	Chairperson
Company:	Community Foundation Board of Directors
File as:	Brooks, Wallace T.
Business Phone:	(504) 555-0138
Home Phone:	(504) 555-0109
Business Fax:	(504) 555-0129
Mobile Phone:	(504) 555-0155
Business Address:	P.O. Box 19039, New Orleans, LA 70115-8329
E-mail:	Wbrooks@cf.org
Web page:	http://www.communityfoundation.org

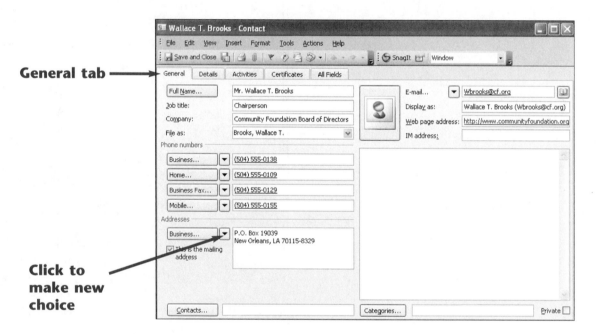

General tab ➝

Click to make new choice ➝

5. Click the *Save and Close* button to save and close this contact.

Create Letter and Envelope Using Contacts List

To create a letter using the contacts list:

1. Click *Contacts* in the Navigation pane. Click the name of the contact you want to send a letter to.

2. On the menu bar, click *Actions*. Choose *New Letter to Contact*. The Letter Wizard displays.

3. Answer the wizard prompts as shown below. Make selections or key data and click *Next* for steps 1, 2, and 3. In step 2, the recipient's name and delivery address data were edited to place the title after the name. The salutation was edited (colon deleted) for open punctuation. In step 4, you will need to key the job title and delete the comma after the closing. Click *Finish* after selecting and entering data in step 4.

Step 1 of 4

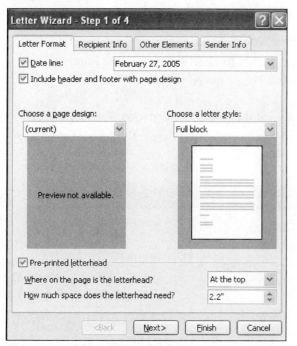

Step 2 of 4

Step 3 of 4

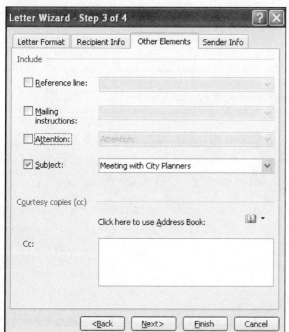

Step 4 of 4

4. Key the letter body shown below. Then proofread and make formatting corrections. For example, add the proper number of blank lines between letter parts and move the enclosure notation below the typist's initials.

Your assistant, Shandra Richardson, was very helpful in rescheduling our 2 p.m. appointment on February 12 to 1 p.m. I appreciate your willingness to share an additional hour with The Sports Connection as we meet with the city planners in finalizing the landscape requirements for the renovation.

The meeting will begin at 1 p.m. in our Conference Room. During this two-hour meeting, we will discuss our landscape plan and will tour the grounds to clarify our position. I am enclosing for your review the landscape plans prepared by our landscape consultants.

5. Now you will create an envelope for the letter. In Word, click *Tools* on the menu bar. Select *Letters and Mailings*. Select *Envelopes and Labels*. The Envelopes and Labels dialog box displays.

Insert Address button

Add to Document button

Omit the return address

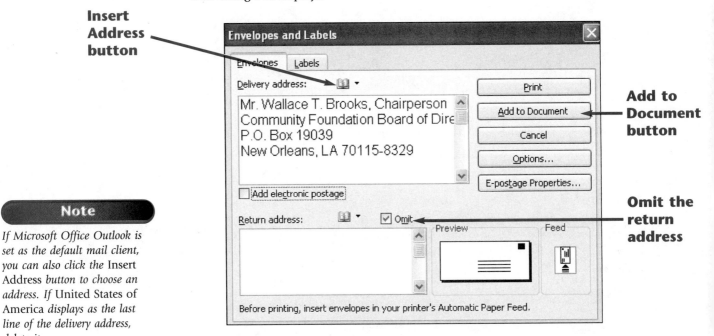

Note

If Microsoft Office Outlook is set as the default mail client, you can also click the Insert Address *button to choose an address. If* United States of America *displays as the last line of the delivery address, delete it.*

6. The address from the letter should appear in the dialog box. Check the *Omit* box by *Return address*, if needed, to omit a return address. Click the *Add to Document* button. The envelope will be inserted at the beginning of the document.

7. Save the document as **Wbrooks (current date),** for example: **Wbrooks 2-27-05.** Print the letter and envelope.

Call Contact Using Automatic Phone Dialing

To automatically dial a number in the contact list:

1. In the Navigation pane, click *Folder List.* Click on the appropriate folder, in this case *Advisory Council.*

2. To select the desired contact:
   a. On the alphabetic index guide at the right of the Contact screen, click the letter that corresponds to the first letter of the last name of the contact (e.g., *B* when looking for Wallace T. Brooks). The insertion point moves to the beginning of the Bs.
   b. Click the contact *Wallace T. Brooks.*

3. Click *Actions* on the menu bar and choose *Call Contact.* Choose the business number. The New Call dialog box displays.

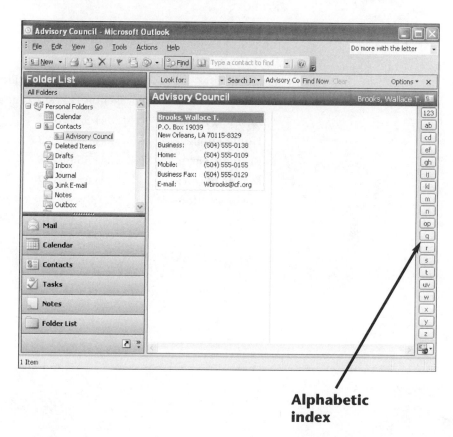

Alphabetic index

Note

If the Create new Journal Entry when starting new call option is selected in the New Call box, a new entry for the Outlook Journal will display. In that case, Ms. McKay can key notes concerning this phone call in the space provided. Be sure to save any Journal entries that are created for later reference.

4. Click the *Start Call* button to initiate the call.

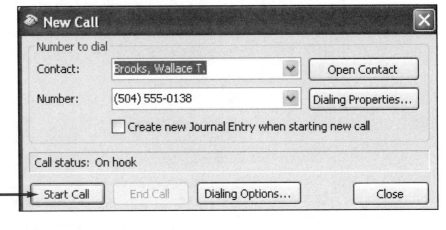

Click to start the call

Practice

1. Add the following contact to the Advisory Council contact folder:

Full name:	Ms. Jill Wikel
Job title:	Marketing Vice President
Company:	Shelton Fitness Company
Business Phone:	(504) 555-0165
Home Phone:	(504) 555-0188
Business Fax:	(504) 555-0198
Mobile Phone:	(504) 555-0107
Business Address:	P.O. Box 3833, New Orleans, LA 70115-3833
Home Address:	1883 West Manchester St., Slidell, LA 70458-1883
E-mail:	jwikel@shelton.com
Web page:	www.shelton.com

2. Save and close the entry.

Create Mail Merge Using Contacts List

Read the directions below to create a mail merge using the contacts list. Then complete the practice exercise.

To create a mail merge using the contacts list:

1. Open the desired Contacts folder (Advisory Council).

2. Click *Tools* on the menu bar and choose *Mail Merge*. The Mail Merge Contacts dialog box displays.

3. Under Document file, select *New document* if a form letter does not exist. Under Merge options, choose *Form Letters* as the Document type. (Notice the other document types that are available.) Under Merge to, choose *New Document*. (Notice the other Merge to options that are available). Click *OK*.

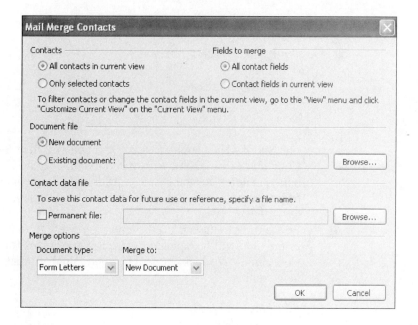

4. A new Word document will open with the Mail Merge toolbar displayed.

5. Create the form file by selecting the desired merge fields. On the Mail Merge toolbar, click the *Insert Merge Fields* button.

6. Select the following fields at the appropriate places in the letter:
   «Full_Name»
   «Job_Title»
   «Company»
   «Business_Address»
   «First_Name»

7. Complete keying the form file. Save the form file with an appropriate name followed by **-frm**. This signals that the letter is a form file.

8. Click the *Merge to New Document* button on the Mail Merge toolbar to merge the contacts and the form file.

9. Save the merged file with an appropriate name followed by **-mrg**. This signals that the form letter is the merged file.

Practice

1. Create the following form letter for the two contacts listed in the Advisory Council Contacts folder. Add appropriate closing notations.

2. Save the form letter as **April 5 meeting-frm**. Save the merged letters as **April 5 meeting-mrg**.

March 31, 200-

«Full_Name», «Job_Title»
«Company»
«Business_Address»

Dear «First_Name»

The Sports Connection Advisory Council will meet on Monday, April 5, at 6 p.m. in the Conference Room. You are invited to come to the Fitness Snack Bar at 5:30 for "healthy" hors d'oeuvres created by our nutrition staff especially for you. The business meeting will begin promptly at 6 p.m. and conclude at 7:30 p.m.

Please refer to the enclosed agenda to review the discussion items. Please note that much of the time will be devoted to discussion of plans for the grand opening of The Sports Connection. We look forward to your valuable input in this important celebration of our new facility.

Sincerely

Karen McKay, Director

xx

Enclosure

Display Map of Address

Often Ms. McKay's appointments are held at the contact's location. To display a map of the contact's address:

1. Open the desired contract (Wallace T. Brooks) by double-clicking the contact. In the Addresses area, choose the type of address (Business, Home, or Other).

2. Click *Actions* on the menu bar and choose *Display Map of Address*. The Web browser opens and then the MSN Maps & Directions Web page opens.

3. Click the appropriate button to get a map or directions. Note that the site cannot display maps or directions for post office box addresses.

Practice

1. Add your name and address as a contact in the Advisory Council contacts folder.

2. Using the directions given above, display a map to your home address. Then display driving directions. For the starting point, enter an address of your choice. Include your address as the ending point.

3. Print the map with turn-by-turn directions.

Index

NOTES

NOTES

NOTES

NOTES

NOTES